Master Storage Spaces Direct (S2D)
Volume 1

Dave Kawula - MVP
Thomas Rayner - MVP
Allan Rafuse - Future MVP
Cristal Kawula – Future MVP

PUBLISHED BY
MVPDays Publishing
http://www.mvpdays.com

Copyright © 2016 by MVPDays Publishing
All rights reserved. No part of this lab manual may be reproduced or transmitted in any form or by any means without the prior written permission of the publisher.
ISBN: 978-1542374712

Warning and Disclaimer

Every effort has been made to make this manual as complete and as accurate as possible, but no warranty or fitness is implied. The information provided is on an "as is" basis. The authors and the publisher shall have neither liability nor responsibility to any person or entity with respect to any loss or damages arising from the information contained in this book.

Feedback Information

We'd like to hear from you! If you have any comments about how we could improve the quality of this book, please don't hesitate to contact us by visiting www.mvpdays.com or sending an email to feedback@mvpdays.com.

Acknowledgements

From Dave

Cristal, you are my rock and my source of inspiration. For the past 20 + years you have been with me every step of the way. Not only are you the "BEST Wife" in the world, you are also my partner in crime. Christian, Trinity, Keira, Serena, Mickaila and Mackenzie, you kids are so patient with your dear old dad when he locks himself away in the office for yet another book. Taking the time to watch you grow in life, sports, and become little leaders of this new world is incredible.

Thank you, Mom and Dad (Frank and Audry). You got me started in this crazy IT world when I was so young. Your efforts helping me review this book are truly appreciated.

I need to throw out a massive thank you in this book to the Storage Team at Microsoft. Your documentation and willingness to share with the community has been amazing. It is your dedication that will help Storage Spaces Direct take off like a rocket. Many of the diagrams and images are courtesy Microsoft Technet.

Last but not least, I'd like to thank the MVPDays volunteers. You have donated your time and expertise and helped us run the event in over 15 cities across North America. Here is to the next 15 events and maybe we will expand to a worldwide roadshow someday.

About the Authors

Dave Kawula - MVP

Dave is a Microsoft Most Valuable Professional (MVP) with over 20 years of experience in the IT industry. His background includes data communications networks within multi-server environments, and he has led architecture teams for virtualization, System Center, Exchange, Active Directory, and Internet gateways. Very active within the Microsoft technical and consulting teams, Dave has provided deep-dive technical knowledge and subject matter expertise on various System Center and operating system topics.

Dave is well-known in the community as an evangelist for Microsoft, 1E, and Veeam technologies. Locating Dave is easy as he speaks at several conferences and sessions each year, including TechEd, Ignite, MVPDays Community Roadshow, and VeeamOn.

As the founder and Managing Principal Consultant at TriCon Elite Consulting, Dave is a leading technology expert for both local customers and large international enterprises, providing optimal guidance and methodologies to achieve and maintain an efficient infrastructure.

BLOG: www.checkyourlogs.net

Twitter: @DaveKawula

Thomas Rayner - MVP

Thomas Rayner is an information technology, entrepreneurship and leadership enthusiast with a penchant for Microsoft tools and products. Thomas is a proud graduate of several programs at NAIT, an institution that he remains actively connected to. He works on the DevOps and Automation team at PCL Construction.

BLOG: http://workingsysadmin.com

Twitter: @mrthomasrayner

Allan Rafuse – Future MVP

Allan has worked as a senior member of the Windows and VMWare Platform Department at Swedbank. He has taken part in the architecture and implementation of multiple datacenters in several countries. He is responsible for the roadmap and lifecycle of the Windows Server

Environment, including the development of ITIL processes for global server OSD, configuration, and performance.

He is an expert at scripting solutions and has an uncanny ability to reduce complexity and maximize the functionality of PowerShell. Allan has recently rejoined the TriCon Elite Consulting team again as a Principal Consultant.

BLOG: http://www.checkyourlogs.net

Twitter: @allanrafuse

Cristal Kawula – Future MVP

Cristal Kawula is the co-founder of MVPDays Community Roadshow and #MVPHour live Twitter Chat. She was also a member of the S2D Technical Advisory board and is the President of TriCon Elite Consulting. Cristal is also only the 2nd woman in the world to receive the prestigious Veeam Vanguard award.

BLOG: http://www.checkyourlogs.net

Twitter: @supercristal1

Technical Editors / Reviewers

Emile Cabot - MVP

Emile started in the industry during the mid-90s working at an ISP and designing celebrity web sites. He has a strong operational background specializing in Systems Management and collaboration solutions, and has spent many years performing infrastructure analyses and solution implementations for organizations ranging from 20 to over 200,000 employees. Coupling his wealth of experience with a small partner network, Emile works very closely with TriCon Elite, 1E, and Veeam to deliver low-cost solutions with minimal infrastructure requirements.

He actively volunteers as a member of the Canadian Ski Patrol, providing over 250 hours each year for first aid services and public education at Castle Mountain Resort and in the community.

BLOG: http://www.checkyourlogs.net

Twitter: @ecabot

Cary Sun – CCIE No. 4531

CISCO CERTIFIED INTERNETWORK EXPERT (CCIE No.4531) and MCSE, MCIPT, Citrix CCA with over fifteen years in the planning, design, and implementation of network technologies and Management and system integration. Background includes hands-on experience with multi-platform, all LAN/WAN topologies, network administration, E-mail and Internet systems, security products, PCs and Servers environment. Expertise analyzing user's needs and coordinating system designs from concept through implementation. Exceptional analysis, organization, communication, and interpersonal skills. Demonstrated ability to work independently or as an integral part of team to achieve objectives and goals.

Kai Poynting

Kai Poynting has over ten years of experience in the technical writing field. as a freelance technical writer, senior technical writer for one of the larger energy software companies in Calgary Alberta, and experience writing about solutions for IT.

In addition to writing about solutions for IT, those ten years were also spent testing, building and deploying some of the same solutions. As part of a small group of consultants, Kai was provided with a great many opportunities to obtain hands on experience in installing, configuring, building, and managing various server solutions, including Server 2008 R2, Exchange 2007 and 2010, Hyper-V, SCVMM, and more. He also provided customer support and technical support for the company's classroom environment, including requirements management, tech support, deployment, and server configuration.

He also holds a BA with an English major, and writes creatively whenever he can. Communication is the cornerstone of his profession and he prides himself on being able to provide the clearest possible message in all documents he provides.

Clint Wyckoff - MVP

Clint Wyckoff is a Technical Evangelist at Veeam with a focus on all things Microsoft. He is an avid technologist and virtualization fanatic with more than a decade of enterprise data center architecture experience. Clint is an energetic and engaging speaker and places a large emphasis on solving the real-world challenges IT professionals face. Additionally, he is a Microsoft Most Valuable Professional (MVP) for Cloud and Datacenter Management as well as a VMware vExpert for 2015 & 2016. Clint is also a Veeam Certified Engineer (VCME) and Microsoft Certified Professional (MCP).

Twitter: @ClintWyckoff.
BLOG: http://cdubhub.us

Contents

Acknowledgements iii
    From Dave iii

About the Authors iv
    Dave Kawula - MVP iv
    Thomas Rayner - MVP iv
    Allan Rafuse – Future MVP iv
    Cristal Kawula – Future MVP v
        Technical Editors / Reviewers v
        Emile Cabot - MVP v
        Cary Sun – CCIE No. 4531 vi
        Kai Poynting vi
        Clint Wyckoff - MVP vi

Contents vii

Introduction 1

What is MVPDays? 1
    North American MVPDays Community Roadshow 1
    Structure of the Book 2
    Sample Files 2
    Additional Resources 2

Chapter 1 1

What is HyperConverged? 1
    History of HyperConverged Infrastructure (HCI) 1
    HyperConverged vs. Converged Infrastructure 2
    Traditional infrastructure was not built for virtualization 3
    HyperConverged Infrastructure 4

Chapter 2 6

Contents

Introducing Storage Spaces Direct (S2D) 6
  Key Benefits of S2D 6
    Simplicity 6
    Performance 7
    Fault Tolerance 7
    Resource Efficiency 7
    Manageability 7
    Scalability 8
  Deployment Options for S2D 9
    Converged 9
    Hyper-Converged 10
  S2D Components 11
    Networking Hardware 12
    Storage Hardware 12
    Failover Clustering 12
    Software Storage Bus 12
    SMB as transport 13
    Software Storage Bus Bandwidth Management 14
    Storage Bus Layer Cache 14
    Storage Pool 14
    Storage Spaces 14
    Resilient File System (ReFS) 14
    Cluster Shared Volumes 15
    Scale-Out File Server 15
  S2D Hardware Requirements 16
    Windows Server Software Defined Program 16
    Basic Requirements 16
    Servers 16
    CPU 17
    Memory 17
    Networking 17
    Drives 17
    Minimum Number of Drives 18
    Maximum Size 18
    Host-bus adapter (HBA) 18
  Fault Tolerance and Efficiency 20
    Mirroring 20
    Two-way mirror 20
    Three-way mirror 21
    Parity – Erasure Coding 21
    Single parity 22
    Dual parity 22
    Local reconstruction codes 23
    When to use parity 24

Contents

    Mixed resiliency 24
    Storage efficiency 24
    S2D Storage Calculator 25
    When to use mixed resiliency 26
  Sample Configurations 27
    Examples where everything stays online 27
    Examples where everything goes offline 29
    Defining Resiliency Settings using PowerShell 29
  S2D Cache 31
    Drive Deployment Options 31
    All-Flash 31
    Hybrid 32
    Cache Drive Selection 32
    Cache behavior 33
    Write-only caching for all-flash deployments 34
    Read/write caching for hybrid deployments 35
    Caching in deployments with drives of all three types 35
  Cache Architecture 36
    Drive bindings are dynamic 36
    Handling cache drive failures 37
    Relationship to other caches 37
    Manual Cache configuration 37
    Set cache behavior 38
    Sizing the cache 39

Chapter 3 42

Windows Server 2016 Failover Clustering 42

  What's new for Windows Server 2016 42
    Cluster operating system rolling upgrades 43
    Storage Replica 44
    Cloud Witness for a Failover Cluster 45
    Fault Domains 45
    Virtual Machine Resiliency 48
    Site-aware Failover Clusters 49
    Workgroup and Multi-domain clusters 49
    VM load balancing 50
    Virtual Machine Start Order 50
    Simplified SMB Multichannel and multi-NIC cluster networks 50
  Diagnostic Improvements 51
    Cluster Log Enhancements 51
    Generating the Cluster.log 51
    What's New in Windows Server 2016 52
    TimeZone Information 53

Cluster Objects	53
Diagnostic Verbose Logging	54
Events from Other Channels	56
Active Memory Dump	57
Configuring Active Memory Dump	58
Health Service	**61**
Prerequisites	61
Metrics	61
Metrics	61
Examples	62
Capacity Planning	62
Faults	63
Fault Coverage	64
Using the Health Service	65
Root Cause Analysis	66
Get-StorageHealthAction	66
Supported Components Document	69
Health Service Settings	71

Chapter 4 73

S2D Networking Primer 73

Windows Server 2016 Network Architecture	74
Teaming Configurations	**74**
Switch-independent teaming	74
Switch-dependent teaming	75
Algorithms for load distribution	76
Converged Network Interface Card (NIC)	77
Switch Independent / Address Hash	78
Switch Independent / Hyper-V Port	78
Switch Independent / Dynamic	78
Switch Embedded Teaming (SET)	**80**
SET Availability	80
SET Supported NICs	81
SET Compatibility	81
SET Modes and Settings	82
Member Adapters	82
Load Balancing Modes for SET	82
SET and Virtual Machine Queues (VMQs)	83
SET and Hyper-V Network Virtualization	83
SET and Live Migration	84
MAC Address Use on Transmitted Packets	84
SET vs. LBFO Teaming	85
Managing SET Teams	86

Contents

    Creating a SET Team 86
    Adding or removing a member of a SET team.. 86
    Removing a SET team 86
    Changing the load distribution algorithm of a SET team.................................. 87
    Forcing the affinity of a VM or vNIC to a physical NIC 87
    Setting up an affinity between a vNIC and a Physical NIC 87
    Checking the affinity between a vNIC and a Physical NIC............................... 88
    Removing the affinity between a vNIC and a Physical NIC 88
  Configuring RDMA for S2D... 89
    Enable Datacenter Bridging (DCB) 90
    Create a Hyper-V Virtual Switch with SET and RDMA vNICs.............................. 91

Chapter 5 92

Deploying Storage Spaces Direct (S2D)...92
    Cisco Nexus 9372x Switch Configuration 100
    Powering on the S2D nodes 103
    IPMI Configuration 103
  Post-Configuration of the S2D Nodes.. 104
  Building a 2-Node S2D Cluster.. 106
    Install Core Windows Roles and features 106
    Configuring Datacenter Bridging 107
    Configuring the SET Team... 108
    Creating RDMA Enabled Virtual Adapters 109
    Verifying RDMA Enabled Virtual Adapters.. 110
    Creating Virtual Adapters for Live Migration and Cluster Heartbeat 111
    Configuring the IP Addresses for the S2D Nodes... 112
    Download and Install all Windows Updates 113
    Validate the Failover Cluster 113
    Build the S2D Failover Cluster 115
    Validate the Cluster prior to Configuring Storage Spaces Direct (S2D)....... 116
    Enable Storage Spaces Direct (S2D).. 116
    Provision Storage Virtual Disks (CSV) 118
    Viewing S2D Volume info with Show Pretty Volume................................... 120
    Expand the Virtual Disk.. 125
    Expand the Pool by adding more disks... 127

Chapter 6 132

Stress testing S2D using VMFleet 132
  Overview of VMFleet Scripts.. 132
    Master Control... 134
  Building VMFleet... 135
    Creating the Cluster Shared Volumes (CSV) for the tests 135

Install the VMFleet Scripts	135
Create the VMFleet Golden Image	136
Create the Fleet VMs	136
Run the VM Fleet	138
Storage QoS	138
Automated Sweeps	139
CPU Target Sweeps	140

Chapter 7 142

Deploying an 8 Node S2D Lab Using Hyper-V 142

Chapter 8 147

Factory Reset of Storage Spaces Direct 147
Clear-SDSConfig.PS1	147

Appendix A 152

BigDemo_S2D Script 152

Find our Experts 168

Join us at MVPDays and meet great MVP's like this in person 168
Live Presentations	168
Video Training	168
Live Instructor-led Classes	168
Consulting Services	169
Twitter	170

Introduction
What is MVPDays?

North American MVPDays Community Roadshow

The purpose of this book is to showcase the amazing expertise of our guest speakers at the North American MVPDays Community Roadshow. They have so much passion, expertise, and expert knowledge that it only seemed fitting to write it down in a book.

MVPDays was founded by Cristal and Dave Kawula back in 2013. It started as a simple idea; "There's got to be a good way for Microsoft MVPs to reach the IT community and share their vast knowledge and experience in a fun and engaging way." We wondered what the point was in recognizing these bright and inspiring individuals, and not leveraging them to inspire the community that they were a part of? If we didn't yet have the right venue to help these individuals inspire and teach, why not create it?

Having established our soapbox, we often get asked the question "Who should attend MVPDays"?

The answer is simple. Anyone that has an interest in technology, is eager to learn, and wants to meet other like-minded individuals should attend. This Roadshow is not just for Microsoft MVP's, but for anyone in the IT Community.

Make sure you check out the MVPDays website at: www.mvpdays.com. You never know, maybe the Roadshow will be coming to a city near you.

The goal of this particular book is to give you some amazing Storage Spaces Direct (S2D) tips from the experts you come to see in person at the MVPDays Roadshow. Each chapter is broken down into a unique tip and we really hope you find immense value in what we have written.

Structure of the Book

Chapter 1 – Introduces the core concepts of HyperConverged Infrastructure

Chapter 2 – Walks through a deep dive on Storage Spaces Direct and all of it's components

Chapter 3 – Is a primer on Windows Server 2016 Clustering. This chapter is especially important as the Window Failover Clustering Services are what provide the high available for Storage Spaces Direct.

Chapter 4 – Networking is the key backbone to any infrastructure and in this chapter we will dive into the new technologies added in Windows Server 2016 that are relevant to Storage Spaces Direct.

Chapter 5 – In this chapter we will build and configure a 2-node Storage Spaces Direct Cluster using physical hardware.

Chapter 6 – Stress testing is an important step required to validate any environment. In this chapter, we will learn about VMFleet from Microsoft and how it can be used perform these stress tests.

Chapter 7 – Now that we have built out a physical Storage Spaces Direct cluster it is time to do it in a Nested Hyper-V environment. We have included as a bonus to this book a script that will deploy your lab with a 16 node Storage Spaces Direct Cluster.

Chapter 8 – So you have completed your lab and want to start over. Wouldn't it be nice to be able to perform a factory like reset in your lab? Well now you can!

Sample Files
All sample files for this book can be downloaded from http://www.checkyourlogs.net and at http://www.github.com/dkawula

Additional Resources
In addition to all tips and tricks provided in this book, you can find extra resources like articles and video recordings on our blog at http://www.checkyourlogs.net.

Chapter 1
What is HyperConverged?

The first HyperConverged systems could be found in the data-centers of web-scale giants such as Facebook and Google. These organizations quickly found that traditional storage architectures did not fit their needs, failing to scale efficiently, and requiring recurring large capital investments and ever-increasing operating expenses. Not to mention, when supporting the rapid expansion required by these web-scale services, it was found to be inefficient to relegate servers to dedicated roles. It was far better to have the same physical server capable of running both compute and storage workloads. As with any vital workload, these services needed to be resilient and highly available. To meet this need, a clustered architecture was deployed.

These web-scale giants quickly realized they could not simply rest on their laurels, and spent accordingly, investing in the required development to make Hyperconvergence a core competency, including the creation of proprietary software. These innovations inevitably drew attention, and found traction in mainstream IT through a slew of imitators entering the market with innovations of their own. These imitators promised the same advantages, improved scalability and lower incremental growth costs, and lower total cost of ownership than the conventional, more rigid architectures of dedicated compute farms and proprietary shared storage systems.

To minimize capital expenditures and operating expenses, industry standard x86 hardware platforms were leveraged, as well as direct-attached storage, rather than purpose-built and proprietary storage systems. The software had to operate both compute workloads and storage on the same hardware, including functions integrated with virtualization hypervisors and operating systems, while still supporting both solid state and rotating storage media.

Organizations of all sizes have benefited from HyperConverged systems as a solution to sprawling server farms, and shared storage systems that are expensive and offer poor scalability. Instead, they are offered a seamless method to integrate multiple sites and hybrid cloud uses.

History of HyperConverged Infrastructure (HCI)

HyperConverged computing was a natural extension rooted in advances in virtualization and the physical shrinking of datacenter hardware. New converged systems were developed by innovative vendors such as HP and IBM, in the form of their HP ConvergedSystem and IBM PurSystem. These were the first examples of companies moving towards what we now know as HCI. Web-scale companies such as, Google, Facebook and Amazon then took the concept several steps further by designing, building and deploying HyperConverged systems in very dense deployments. Google was a pioneer in the area of the modular datacenters built from shipping containers containing racks of HyperConverged systems. This container approach carried the modular characteristics of the HCI to the next level, as those shipping containers could also be stacked and quickly connected to a datacenter network. This approach created large-scale modular computing environments based on small-scale modular computing systems.

Microsoft also started to invest heavily in this area of HCI with their own version, called Storage Spaces Direct. This technology will soon be adopted into the modular datacenters used for Azure around the world. Below is an image of one such Microsoft container based HyperConverged datacenters in Chicago.

Figure 1 - Microsoft HyperConverged modular datacenter in a container

HyperConverged vs. Converged Infrastructure

HyperConverged systems grew out of the market movement for converged systems, which features individual components specifically designed to inter-operate seamlessly. HCI takes that idea to the next level by combining those individual components into a single chassis, allowing for even tighter integration between the storage, compute, network and management software. The result is a modular datacenter building block, with each HyperConverged system able to be deployed and configured very quickly. Some HCI vendors offer to load disk images and pre-configure the HyperConverged system so that it can literally be slid into a rack, plugged into power and network, turned on and be operating very quickly. HCS provides key advantages over converged systems, including speed of deployment, ease of installation, and rapid utility.

Traditional infrastructure was not built for virtualization

The powers of virtualization and, increasingly, cloud computing have been central to accelerating innovation. IT Professionals can now spin up new logical servers in minutes rather than the weeks or months it took to physically deploy new hardware.

However, virtualization has until now been layered on top of traditional infrastructure. What this means is that datacenters have achieved a level of unparalleled utility and functionality – but at the same time these technologies have created an age of unprecedented complexity. Even without virtualization, IT's administrative burden has been growing rapidly. New generations of hardware of ever-increasing sophistication need to be configured and deployed every few months.

Virtualization multiplies this burden exponentially. On top of configuring each component, each virtual machine must be provisioned with storage, compute, power and networking. The result: over the last 10 years, while server hardware costs have actually declined, virtualization led to the number of logical servers quadrupling and to administrative costs tripling.

The driving force behind this cost is the complexity of the underlying infrastructure. The traditional three tiers of infrastructure create a series of silos and integration points between the various layers of compute, the storage area network, and the underlying storage. All of these silos and integration points need to be managed as if they were a single resource, and presented to the hypervisors. As these environments grow, the underlying complexity of these management and integration points grows exponentially.

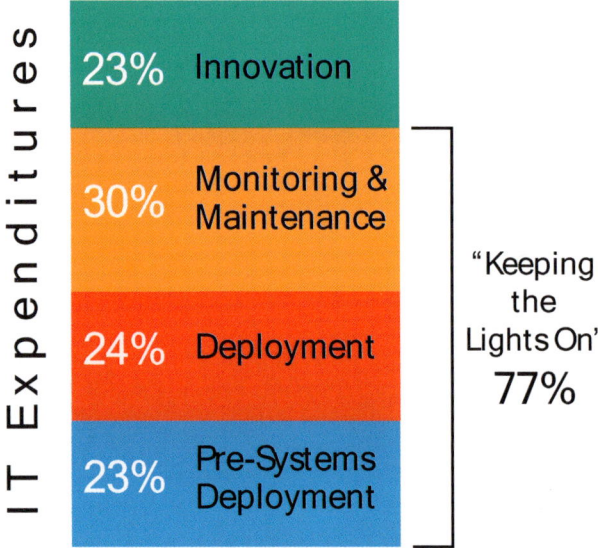

Figure 2 - 2013 IDC study of the typical IT Budget

It has now reached the point that administrative costs are crowding out innovations. According to a 2013 IDC study, just keeping the lights on (systems planning, deploying, maintaining) takes up 77% of IT's budget while only 23% goes to supporting business innovation. The major component causing this undue burden is the mismatch of layering virtualization on top of the traditional infrastructure that was never designed for this task.

HyperConverged Infrastructure

The key to hyper-scale datacenters, characterized by unprecedented scale, economics, and efficiency, is simplicity and a software layer that aggregates compute and storage resources from many standard x86 building blocks into one massive resource. Intelligent software automates the provisioning and control of resources to each workload.

This approach to infrastructure has become widely known as HyperConverged. Three layers of traditional infrastructure are consolidated into a single tier build from x86 building blocks and intelligent software that automates everything. Eliminating layers of infrastructure results in:

- **Reduced capital costs:** Two of the three infrastructure layers are effectively eliminated.
- **Reduced management effort:** Less infrastructure means less to manage and a geometric reduction in discrete management points between discrete infrastructure components.

- **Reduced operating costs**: Reducing management effort frees staff for value-added activities. Decreasing infrastructure with the potential to break reduces management requirements. Reduced space, power and cooling all combine to drive down the costs of operations.
- **Reduced operating risk:** Rather than risking being concentrated within an infrastructure silo, HyperConverged architectures are designed to expect many component failures. By using standard components as shared resources, the system simply works around faults and self-heals using added x86 building blocks.

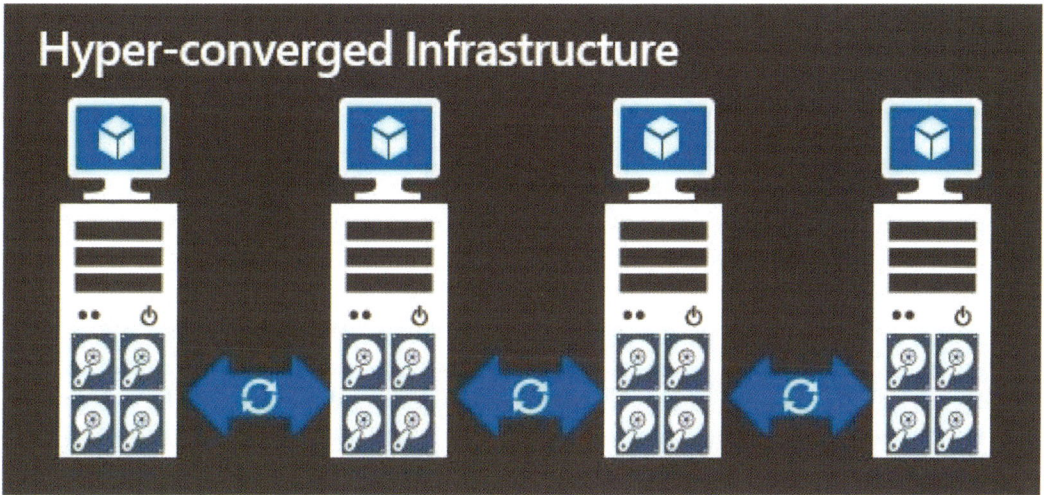

Figure 3 – HyperConverged Infrastructure Illustraiton

Chapter 2
Introducing Storage Spaces Direct (S2D)

Using industry-standard servers and local-attached drives, Storage Spaces Direct creates highly available, scalable, and cost-friendly software-defined storage. At a fraction of the cost of traditional SAN or NAS arrays, their converged or hyper-converged architecture thoroughly simplifies procurement and deployment. Hardware innovation such as RDMA networking and NVMe drives, along with features such as storage tiers, caching, and erasure coding, deliver unparalleled efficiency and performance.

Key Benefits of S2D

There are several key benefits of Storage Spaces Direct including:
- Simplicity
- Performance
- Fault Tolerance
- Resource Efficiency
- Manageability
- Scalability

Simplicity

In this book, you will see how simple and easy it is to take a set of Windows Server 2016 Servers and configure S2D. A basic configuration can be performed in less than 15 minutes. Microsoft has done a great job with their pre-configured PowerShell Cmdlets like Enable-ClusterS2D.

Performance

S2D can be configured in a variety of ways including (but not limited to):
- All-Flash using NVMe Drives
- All-Flash using traditional SSD Drives
- Hybrid using NVMe + SSD
- Hybrid using SSD + HDD

Regardless of the selected configuration S2D can easily exceed 150,000 mixed 4K random IOPS per server. This is because Microsoft uses a hypervisor-embedded architecture.

Fault Tolerance

S2D offers built-in resiliency and can easily handle drive, server, or component failures with continuous availability. It has support for chassis or rack aware fault domains which is a critical component for enterprise customers. If hardware does fail simply replace it and S2D will automatically self-heal.

Resource Efficiency

Erasure coding delivers up to 2.4x greater storage efficiency, with unique innovations like Local Reconstruction Codes and real-time tiering to extend these gains to hard disk drives and mixed hot/cold workloads, all while minimizing CPU consumption to give resources back to where they're needed most – the VMs.

Manageability

You can use Storage Quality of Service (QoS) to keep the overly busy VMs throttled down. This can be configured with a minimum and maximum per VM IOPS limit. Continuous built-in monitoring and alerting is provided by the Health Service, and new APIs help to easily collect rich, cluster-wide performance and capacity metrics. Vendors such as DataON have used this Health Service to build a rich monitoring UI for S2D.

Scalability

At the time of writing, S2D can be configured to support up to 16 nodes and over 400 drives. This equates a maximum supportability of multiple petabytes per cluster. To scale out the infrastructure, S2D will automatically onboard new drives and begin using them.

Chapter 2   Introducing Storage Spaces Direct (S2D)

Deployment Options for S2D

S2D can be configured in a Converged or Hyper-Converged design.   These deployment options are shown below:

Converged

The converged deployment option layers a Scale-Out File Server (SoFS) on top of S2D providing access to Virtual Machines via SMB3 file shares.   This allows for scaling compute and workloads independently of the storage cluster.   This design is critical for larger customers like hosting providers that need to scale all of their infrastructure independently and reduce maintenance windows.

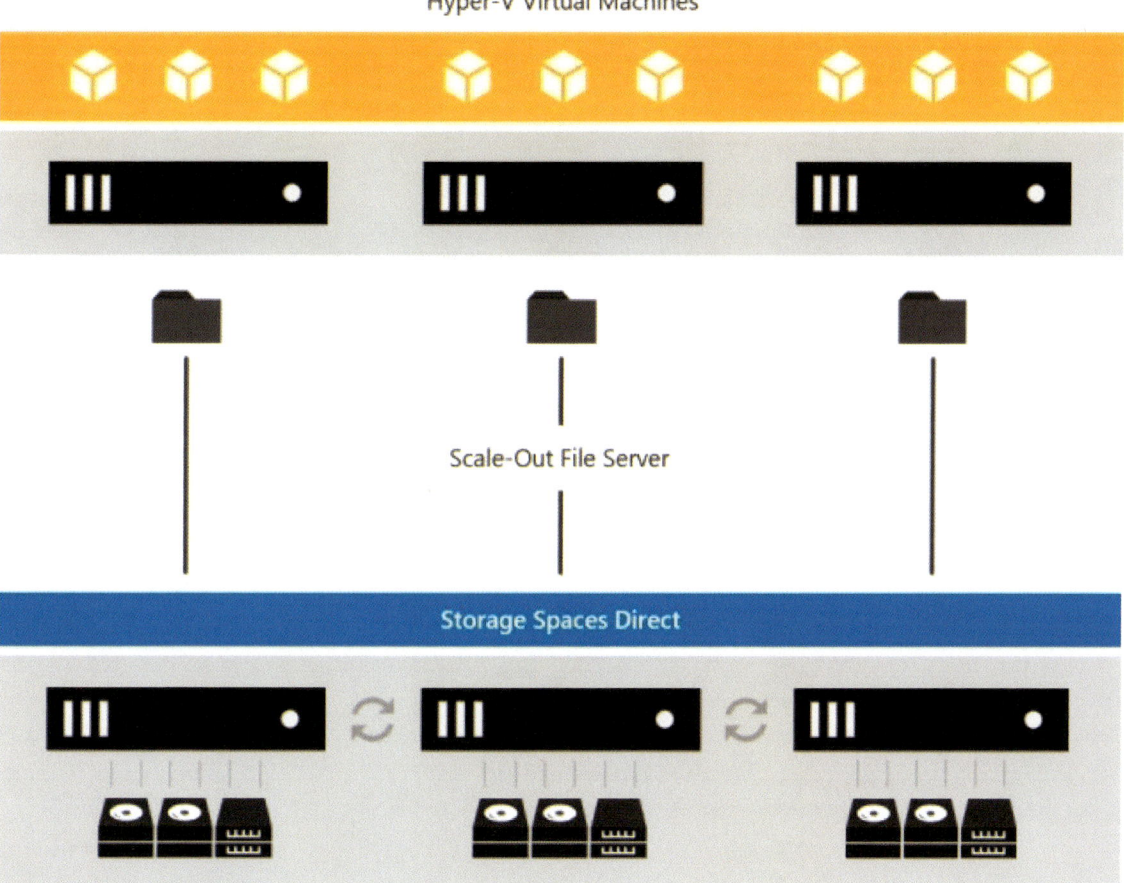

Figure 5 – Converged S2D Design

Hyper-Converged

The hyper-converged deployment option consists of Hyper-V virtual machines or SQL Server databases running directly on the servers providing the storage. This configuration reduces hardware costs, and effectively eliminates the need to configure file server access and permissions.

> **Note**: Hyper-Converged infrastructure can be more expensive from an operational perspective. Maintenance windows are significantly longer and the tiers are collapsed. Careful consideration and planning is required whenever looking into a hyper-converged solution. From our experience the maintenance windows for patching a hyper-converged cluster can be 2-4x longer than a traditional dis-aggregated converged cluster.

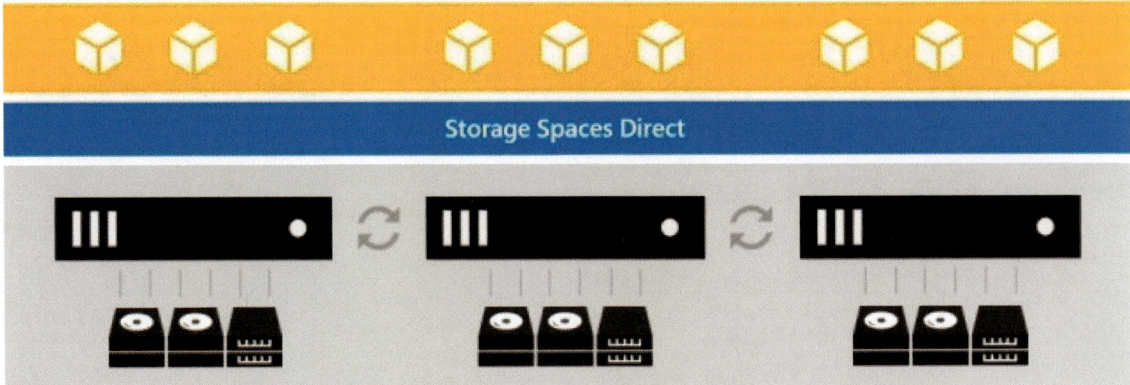

Figure 5 – S2D Hyper-Converged Design

S2D Components

Storage Spaces Direct is a direct descendant of Microsoft's Storage Spaces, introduced in Windows 2012. It leverages many of the features that are currently used in Windows Server, such as Failover Clustering, Cluster Shared Volumes (CSV) file system, Server Message Block (SMB) 3, and of course Storage Spaces. It also introduces new technology, most notably the Software Storage Bus.

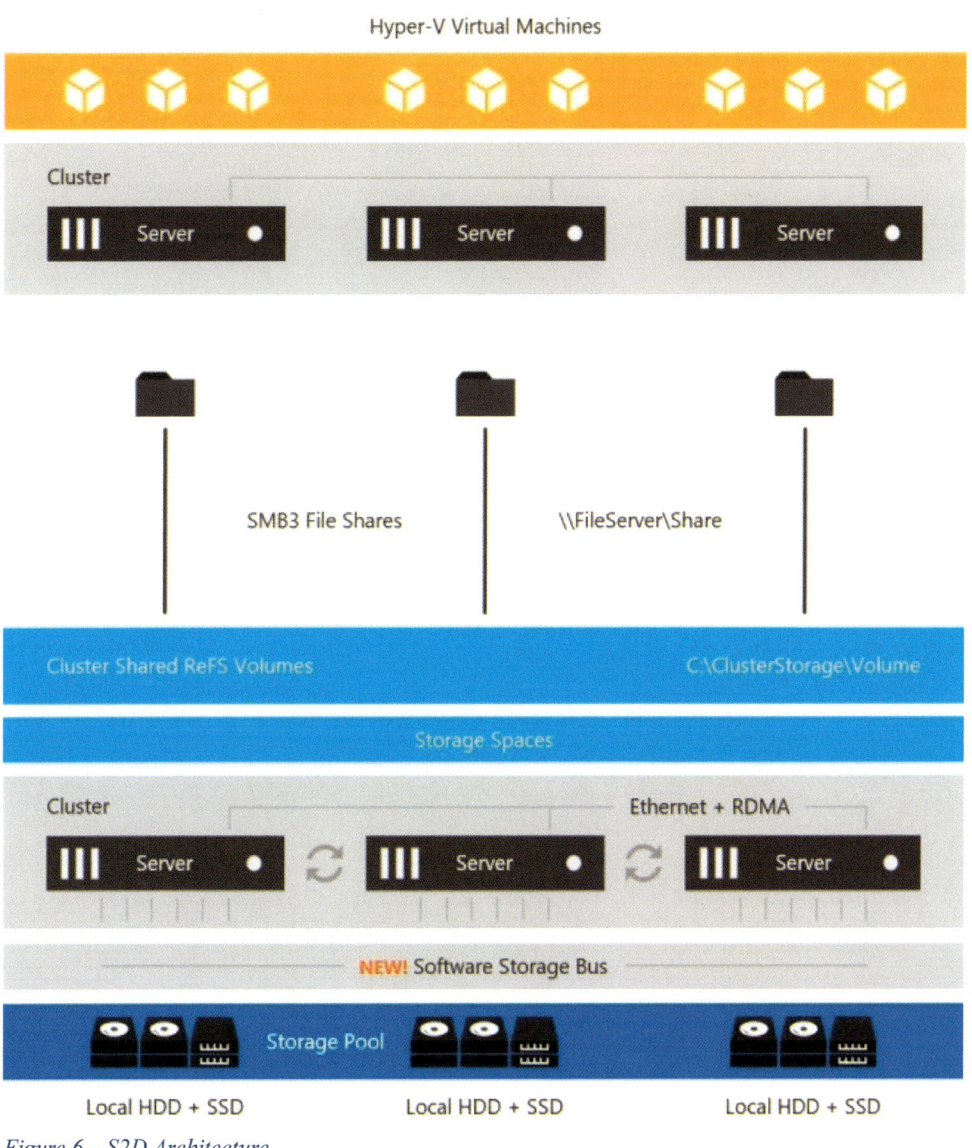

Figure 6 – S2D Architecture

Networking Hardware

S2D uses SMB3, including SMB Direct and SMB Multichannel, over Ethernet to communicate between servers. Microsoft strongly recommends to use 10+ GbE with remote-direct memory access (RDMA) with either iWARP or RoCE to achieve the best performance.

Storage Hardware

S2D can be configured with as few as 2 Servers and as many as 16 Servers. These Servers can be provisioned with local-attached SATA, SAS, or NVMe drives. Each of these servers must have at least 2 solid state drives, and at least 4 additional drives. For best performance, the SATA and SAS devices should be behind a host-bus adapter (HBA) and SAS expander.

Failover Clustering

The built-in Failover Clustering provided by Windows Server 2016 is used to connect the servers together in a highly available configuration.

Software Storage Bus

The Software Storage Bus is a virtual storage bus spanning all of the servers that make up the cluster. Software Storage Bus essentially ensures visibility between each server, allowing them to see all disks across all servers in the cluster, providing full mesh connectivity. Two components make up the Software Storage Bus on each server in the cluster:

- **ClusPort**
    - ClusPort implements a virtual host bus adapter (HBA) that allows the node to connect to disk devices in all the other servers in the cluster.
- **ClusBlft**
    - ClusBlft implements virtualization of the disk devices and enclosures in each server for ClusPort in other servers to connect to.

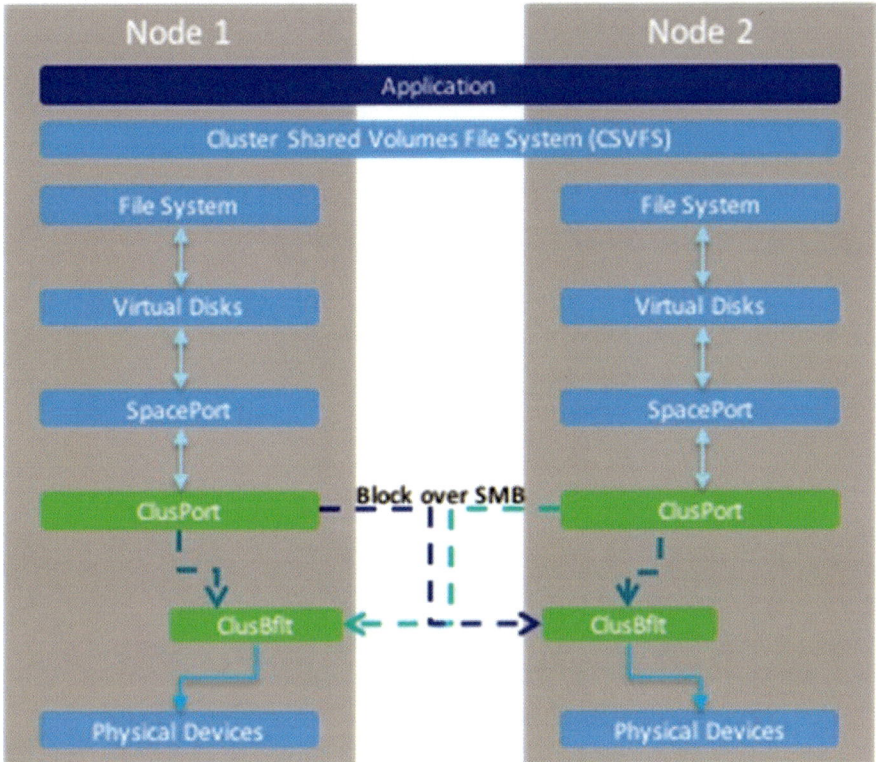

Figure 7 – The Software Storage Bus

SMB as transport

Communication for the Software Storage Bus is transported between servers in the cluster using SMB3 and SMB Direct. A separate named instance of SMB3 is used by the Software Storage Bus, separating it from other consumers of SMB, such as CSVFS, to provide additional resiliency. By leveraging SMB3, the SoftWare Storage Bus can take advantage of innovations such as SMB Multichannel and SMB direct.

SMB Multichannel can improve throughput and resiliency to a failed network interface by aggregating bandwidth across multiple network interfaces.

SMB Direct can dramatically lower the CPU overhead of doing IO over the network and reduce the latency to disk devices by using RDMA enabled network adapters, including iWARP and RoCE.

Software Storage Bus Bandwidth Management

The Software Storage Bus also ensures fair device access, preventing any one server from starving out the others, using a fair access algorithm. Another algorithm prioritizes Application IO, which usually is IO from virtual machines, over system IO, which usually would be rebalance or repair operations. This algorithm, though it prioritizes Application IO, still ensures that rebalance and repair operations can make forward progress.

Storage Bus Layer Cache
The Software Storage Bus dynamically binds the fastest drives present to slower drives to provide server-side read/write caching that accelerates IO and boosts throughput.

Storage Pool
A storage pool is a collection of drives aggregated to form the basis of Storage Spaces. The storage pool is automatically created, and all eligible drives within the cluster are automatically discovered and added to it. One pool per cluster, with default settings, is Microsoft's strong recommendation.

Storage Spaces
Fault tolerance for your virtual disks in Storage Spaces is based on mirroring, erasure coding, or both. Essentially, virtual drives in Storage Spaces behave as if using distributed, software defined RAID. In Storage Spaces Direct, these fault tolerant virtual disks can typically survive two simultaneous drive failures. This configuration is also known as 3-way mirroring.

Resilient File System (ReFS)
ReFS is the premier filesystem purpose-built for virtualization. It includes dramatic accelerations for .vhdx file operations such as creation, expansion, checkpoint merging, and provides built-in checksums to detect and correct bit errors (BitRot). It also introduces real-time tiers that rotate data between hot and cold storage tiers in real-time based on usage.

Cluster Shared Volumes

The CSV file system unifies all the ReFS volumes into a single namespace accessible through any server, so that to each server, every volume looks and acts like it is mounted locally.

Scale-Out File Server

This final layer is necessary in converged deployments only. It provides remote file access using the SMB3 access protocol to clients, such as another cluster running Hyper-V, over the network, effectively turning Storage Spaces Direct into network attached storage (NAS).

S2D Hardware Requirements

This topic describes minimum hardware requirements for testing Storage Spaces Direct.

> Be very careful when designing a S2D configuration as not all hardware is compatible. For example, your RAID Controller must be configured as a SAS HBA. If not your drives will show up as an unsupported configuration. Microsoft highly recommends sticking to the solution offerings from vendors in the Windows Server Software Defined program. Each of these has been tested and verified to work with S2D. Although your custom configuration will likely work, if it is something that has not been thoroughly tested by Microsoft, your results may vary when compared to published documents with certified solutions.

Windows Server Software Defined Program

For production environments, Microsoft recommends acquiring a Windows Server Software-Defined hardware/software offering, which includes production deployment tools and procedures. These offerings are designed, assembled, and validated to meet Microsoft's requirements for private cloud environments, helping ensure stable operation.

Basic Requirements

All systems, components, devices, and drivers must be "Certified for Windows Server 2016" per the Windows Server Catalog.

The fully configured cluster (servers, networking, and storage) must pass all the cluster validation tests per the wizard in the Failover Cluster snap-in or with the **Test-Cluster** cmdlet in PowerShell.

Servers

- Minimum of 2 servers with a maximum of 16 servers
- All servers must be identical in hardware, components, drivers, firmware, and configuration

CPU

- Minimum of Intel Nehalem or later compatible processor

Memory

- 5 gigabytes (GB) of memory per terabyte (TB) of cache drive on each server, to store metadata structures. For example, if each server has 2 x 1 TB cache drives, you should have 2 x 5 GB = 10 GB of memory for Storage Spaces Direct internal use.
- Any memory needed for your applications or workloads

Networking

- Minimum of 10 Gbps network interface for intra-cluster communication
- Recommended: Two NICs for redundancy and performance
- Recommended: Interfaces which are remote-direct memory access (RDMA) capable, iWARP, or RoCE

Drives

- Local-attached SATA, SAS, or NVMe Drives
- Every drive must be physically connected to only one server
- Ensure SSDs are "Enterprise-grade", meaning they have power-loss protection
- Ensure SSDs used for cache have high write endurance. We recommend 5+ drive-writes-per-day (DWPD)
- Drives can be 512n, 512e, or 4K native, all work equally well
- Separate dedicated drive for boot /system partitions

- Not Supported: multi-path IO (MPIO) or physically connecting drives via multiple paths

Minimum Number of Drives

- If there are drives used as cache, there must be at least 2 per server
- There must be at least 4 non-cache drives per server

Drive types present	Minimum number required
All NVMe (Same Model)	4 NVMe
All SSD (Same Model)	4 SSD
NVMe + SSD	2 NVMe + 4 SSD
NVMe + HDD	2 NVMe + 4 HDD
SSD + HDD	2 SSD + 4 HDD
NVMe + SSD + HDD	2 NVMe + 4 other

Maximum Size

- Maximum of 1 petabyte (1,000 TB) of raw capacity per storage pool

Host-bus adapter (HBA)

- Simple pass-through SAS HBA for both SAS and SATA drives
- SCSI Enclosure Services (SES) for SAS and SATA drives
- Any direct-attached storage enclosures must present a Unique ID
- Not Supported: RAID HBA Controllers or SAN (Fibre Channel, iSCSI, or FCoE) devices

Chapter 2 Introducing Storage Spaces Direct (S2D)

Fault Tolerance and Efficiency

Fault tolerance, or resiliency, is core to Storage Spaces Direct. Your data must be available at all times, and free of corruption. In Storage Spaces Direct, fault tolerance performs much like RAID, save it is distributed across servers, and implemented as software.

As with RAID, Storage Spaces can handle fault tolerance in a few different ways, each with different tradeoffs between fault tolerance, storage efficiency, and compute complexity. These options broadly fall into two categories: 'mirroring' and 'parity', the latter sometimes called 'erasure coding'.

Mirroring

Mirroring provides fault tolerance by keeping multiple copies of all data. This most closely resembles RAID-1. Like RAID-1, any data stored using Storage Spaces Direct mirroring is written, in its entirety, multiple times. This data is striped and placed using a non-trivial algorithm. Each copy is written to spread across different physical hardware (different drives in different servers) which are assumed to fail independently.

> **Note:** In Windows Server 2016, Storage Spaces offers two flavors of mirroring – 'two-way' and 'three-way'.

Two-way mirror

Two-way mirroring writes two copies of everything. This also means that storage efficiency is 50% - for each terabyte of data, you will need at least 2 terabytes of storage capacity. You will also need two hardware 'fault domains'. In Storage Spaces Direct, this is defined as two separate servers.

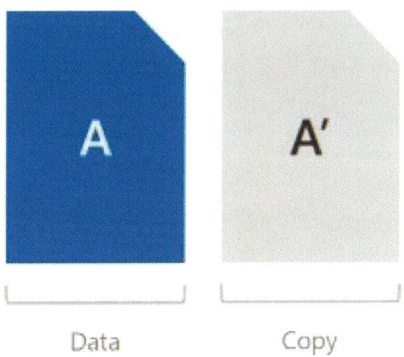

Figure 8 – Two-Way Mirror

Three-way mirror

Three-way mirroring writes three copies of everything. As you probably guessed, storage efficiency in a three-way mirror is 33.3% – for each terabyte of data, you need at least 3 terabytes of physical storage capacity. Likewise, you will need at least three hardware 'fault domains' – meaning your data will be spread across three servers.

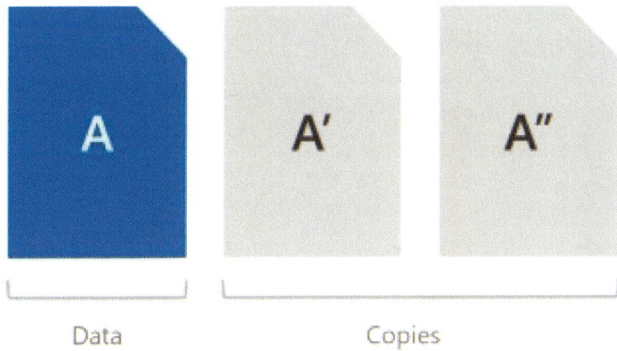

Figure 9 – Three-Way Mirror

Whichever mirroring flavor you choose, it will provide the fastest possible reads and writes, with the least complexity. This ensures the least latency and compute overhead. It is the best option for acutely performance-sensitive workloads or when vast amounts of data are being actively, randomly written, so-called "hot" data. The downside to mirroring is its lesser storage efficiency.

Parity – Erasure Coding

Parity encoding, sometimes referred to as 'erasure coding', uses bitwise arithmetic to provide fault tolerance to your data. The calculations can get remarkably complicated. The way this works is less obvious than mirroring, but suffice it to say it provides better storage efficiency without compromising fault tolerance.

Windows Server 2016 offers two types of parity - 'single' parity and 'dual' parity. The latter employs an advanced technique called 'local reconstruction codes' at larger scales.

Single parity

Because single parity keeps only one bitwise parity symbol, it provides fault tolerance against only one failure at a time. It most closely resembles RAID-5. To use single parity, you need at least three hardware fault domains, or, in Storage Spaces Direct, three servers. Because three-way mirroring provides more fault tolerance at the same scale, we discourage using single parity. We feel that any gain in storage efficiency does not adequately mitigate the reduced fault-tolerance. But, it is available if you insist on using it, and it is fully supported.

> **Note:** This is also known in the industry as a 2+1 configuration. Microsoft strongly discourages people from using this configuration as it can only safely tolerate one hardware failure at a time. If you are rebooting one server, and a drive fails in another server, you will experience downtime. If you only have three servers, we recommend using three-way mirroring. If you have four or more, see the next section.

Dual parity

Dual parity implements Reed-Solomon error-correcting codes to keep two bitwise parity symbols, thereby providing the same fault tolerance as three-way mirroring (i.e. up to two failures at once), but with better storage efficiency. It most closely resembles RAID-6. At least four hardware fault domains are required for dual parity (or four servers in S2D). Storage Efficiency at this minimum scale is 50%, meaning for every 2 TB of data, 4 TB of physical storage capacity is required. Effectively, this provides the fault-tolerance of a three-way mirror, with the storage efficiency of a two way mirror.

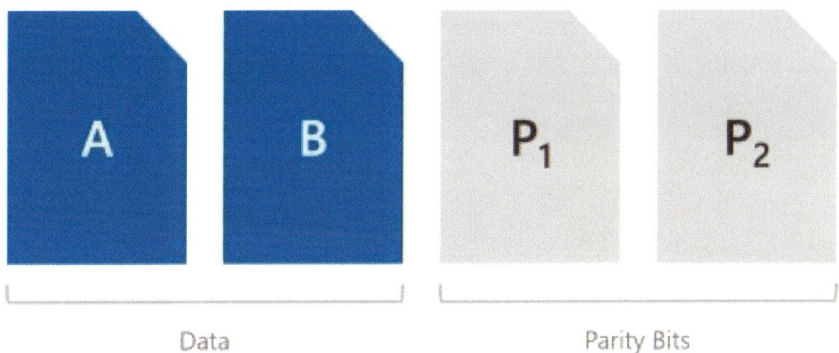

Figure 10 – Dual Parity

However, dual parity is not limited to this minimum. Storage efficiency increases the more hardware fault domains are integrated, from 50% up to 80%. For example, at seven (with Storage Spaces Direct, that means seven servers) the efficiency jumps to 66.7% – or in other words, to store 4 TB of data, you need just 6 TB of physical storage capacity.

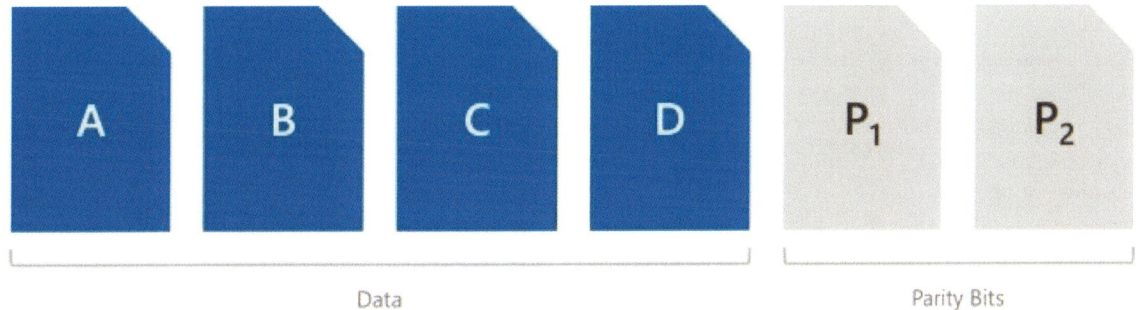

Figure 11 – Increased Dual Parity with more Hardware

Note: In the industry, this is known as a 4+2 configuration.

Local reconstruction codes

'Local reconstruction codes', or LRC is an advanced technique developed by Microsoft Research and introduced in Storage Spaces in Windows Server 2016. For large scale deployments using dual parity, LRC is used to split its encoding/decoding into a few smaller groups, reducing the overhead required to make writes or recover from failures.

With hard disk drives (HDD) the group size is four symbols; with solid-state drives (SSD), the group size is six symbols. For example, here's what the layout looks like with hard disk drives and 12 hardware fault domains (meaning 12 servers). As you can see, there are two groups of four data symbols. This configuration achieves a 72.7% storage efficiency.

When to use parity

Parity provides far better storage efficiency than mirroring, but this comes at the expense of complexity and compute overhead. Fault recovery, or even simply writing data, incurs encoding and decoding operations. Because of this compute overhead, parity is best suited for infrequently written, so-called "cold" data, and data which is written in bulk, such as archival or backup workloads.

Mixed resiliency

With the advent of Windows Server 2016, Storage Spaces Direct now supports volumes that can be part mirror and part parity. The new Resilient File System is able to intelligently move data between the two resiliency types in real-time, based on read/write activity. Active data is kept in the mirroring part of the volume. This provides the best of both worlds, improved performance and faster writes for 'hot' data, and better storage efficiency for your infrequently accessed 'colder' data.

To mix three-way mirror and dual parity, you need at least four fault domains, meaning four servers.

Storage efficiency

The storage efficiency of mixed resiliency is, as you might expect, somewhere between what you would get if using an all mirror, or all parity configuration. The storage efficiency depends strongly on the proportions you choose. A 12 server configuration can provide storage efficiencies ranging anywhere from 46 to 65% dependent on the amount of mirroring and parity used in the configuration.

S2D Storage Calculator

Microsoft has provided a storage calculator to help you decide on the right configuration for you. The beta S2D storage calculator can be found at http://www.cosmosdarwin.com/spacesdirect/.

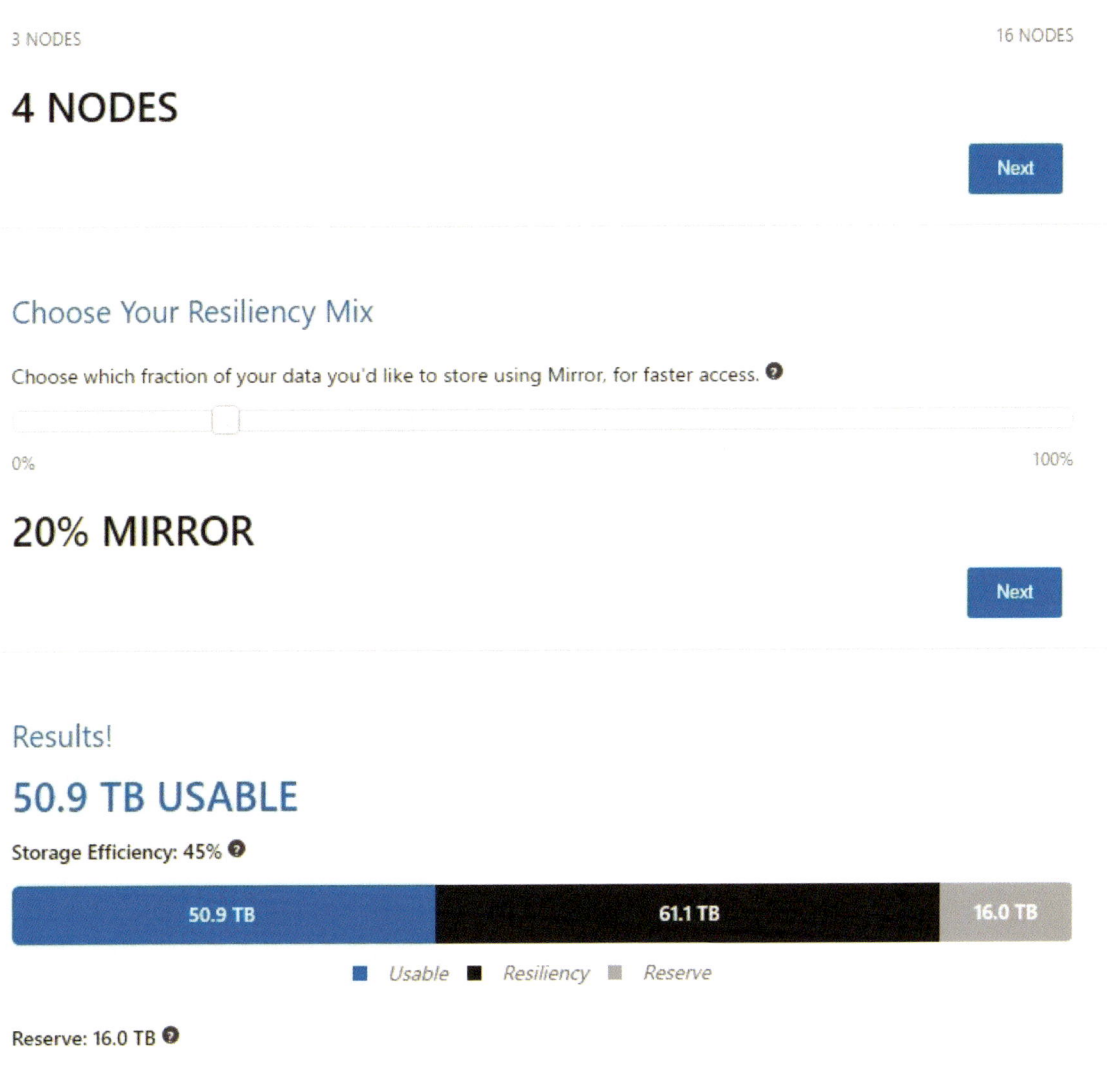

Figure 12 – S2D Calculator

When to use mixed resiliency

Consider using mixed resiliency when most of your data is "cold" data, but you still expect some sustained write activity to a portion of your data.

Sample Configurations

Unless you have only two servers, we recommend using three-way mirroring and/or dual parity, because they offer better fault tolerance. Specifically, they ensure that all data remains safe and continuously accessible even when two fault domains – with Storage Spaces Direct, that means two servers - are affected by simultaneous failures.

Examples where everything stays online

These six examples show what three-way mirroring and/or dual parity can tolerate.

1. One drive lost (includes cache drives)
2. One server lost

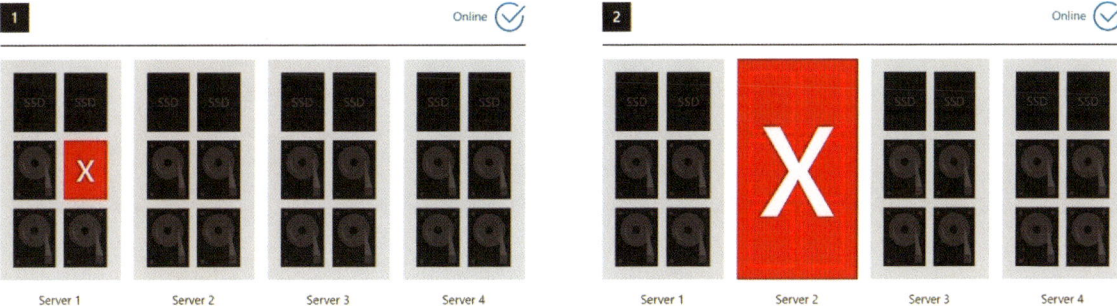

Figure 13 – One lost drive or Node

3. One server and one drive lost
4. Two drives lost in different servers

Chapter 2   Introducing Storage Spaces Direct (S2D)

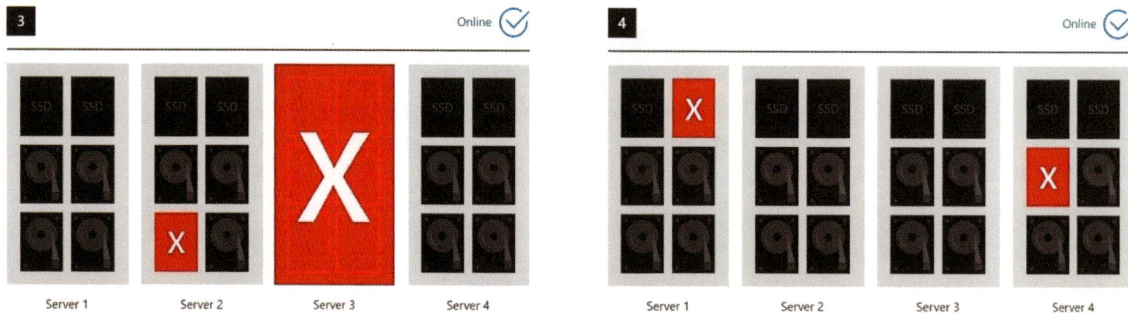

Figure 14 – Two Lost Drives or One Drive and One Node

5. More than two drives lost, so long as at most two servers are affected
6. Two servers lost

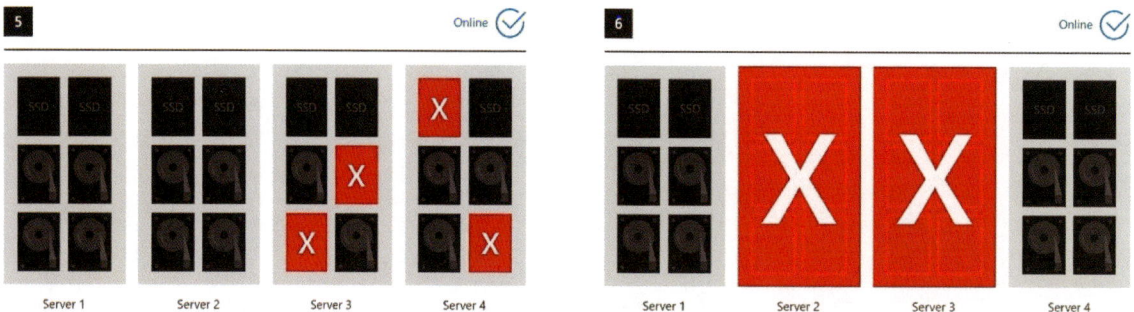

Figure 15 – More than one Drive in a single Node or 2 full Nodes

> **Note:** As long as the cluster can maintain quorum everything will remain online in the above examples.

Examples where everything goes offline

Over its lifetime, Storage Spaces can tolerate any number of failures, because it restores to full resiliency after each one, given sufficient time. However, at most two fault domains can safely be affected by failures at any given moment. The following are therefore examples of what three-way mirroring and/or dual parity cannot tolerate.

7. Drives lost in three or more servers at once

8. Three or more servers lost at once

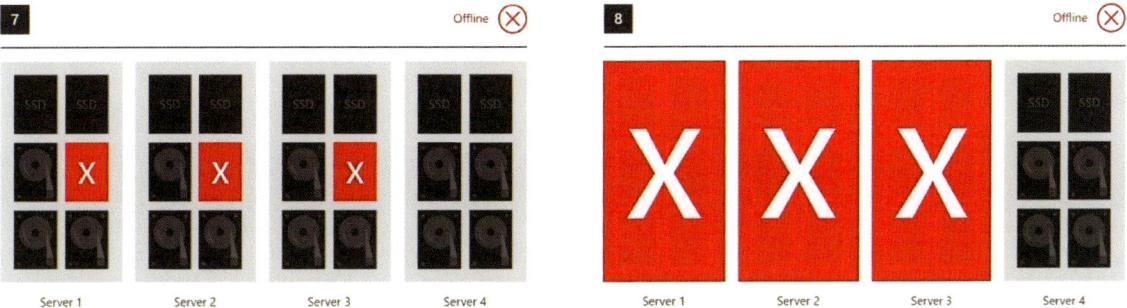

Figure 16 – Everything Goes offline

Defining Resiliency Settings using PowerShell

When you create volumes ("Storage Spaces"), you can specify which resiliency type to use. To configure your volume in PowerShell, simply use the **New-Volume** cmdlet, and its associated **ResiliencySettingName** and **PhysicalDiskRedundancy** parameters.

In the below example, each of the four cmdlets create a volume. Mirror 1 uses two-way mirror; Mirror 2 uses three-way mirror; Parity 1 uses single parity; and Parity 2 uses dual parity. Provided the minimum number of fault domains (servers) are available for each option, these cmdlets are the most prescriptive and surefire way to create exactly the configuration you want. When using these cmdlets, don't forget to specify the **FriendlyName** and **Size** you want.

```
New-Volume -FriendlyName "Mirror 1" -FileSystem CSVFS_ReFS -StoragePoolFriendlyName S2D* -Size 1TB -ResiliencySe
ttingName Mirror -PhysicalDiskRedundancy 1
New-Volume -FriendlyName "Mirror 2" -FileSystem CSVFS_ReFS -StoragePoolFriendlyName S2D* -Size 1TB -ResiliencySe
ttingName Mirror -PhysicalDiskRedundancy 2
New-Volume -FriendlyName "Parity 1" -FileSystem CSVFS_ReFS -StoragePoolFriendlyName S2D* -Size 1TB -ResiliencySe
ttingName Parity -PhysicalDiskRedundancy 1
New-Volume -FriendlyName "Parity 2" -FileSystem CSVFS_ReFS -StoragePoolFriendlyName S2D* -Size 1TB -ResiliencySe
ttingName Parity -PhysicalDiskRedundancy 2
```

To make things easier, if your deployment uses Storage Spaces Direct with only two or three servers, you can omit the **ResiliencySettingName** and **PhysicalDiskRedundancy** parameters altogether, and Storage Spaces will automatically use the most fault tolerant mirroring option.

```
New-Volume -FriendlyName "Bill Gates" -FileSystem CSVFS_ReFS -StoragePoolFriendlyName S2D* -Size 1TB
```

For deployments using four or more servers, Storage Spaces Direct automatically creates what are referred to as 'tier templates', called Performance and Capacity. These templates define the best configurations for three-way mirroring (Performance), and the best dual parity configurations (Capacity) at your scale. If you are curious, run the below cmdlet to see them running.

```
Get-StorageTier | Select FriendlyName, ResiliencySettingName, PhysicalDiskRedundancy
```

```
Administrator: Windows PowerShell
Windows PowerShell
Copyright (C) 2016 Microsoft Corporation. All rights reserved.

PS C:\> Get-StorageTier | Select FriendlyName, ResiliencySettingName, PhysicalDiskRedundancy

FriendlyName         ResiliencySettingName  PhysicalDiskRedundancy
------------         ---------------------  ----------------------
Capacity             Parity                                      2
Performance          Mirror                                      2


PS C:\>
```

Figure 17 – Get-StorageTier

These tier templates can be referenced when creating volumes, particularly mixed resiliency volumes, by using the **StorageTierFriendlyNames** and **StorageTierSizes** parameters. The cmdlet below will provision a 1 TB mixed volume, divided into a 30% three-way mirror and 70% dual parity configuration.

```
New-Volume -FriendlyName "Sir-Mix-A-Lot" -FileSystem CSVFS_ReFS -StoragePoolFriendlyName S2D* -StorageTierFriend
lyNames Performance, Capacity -StorageTierSizes 300GB, 700GB
```

S2D Cache

S2D features a built-in server-side cache to maximize storage performance. It is a large, persistent, real-time read and write cache. The cache is configured automatically when Storage Spaces Direct is enabled. In most cases, no manual management is required. How the cache works depends on the configuration.

Drive Deployment Options

S2D currently works with three types of drives:

Figure 17 – Drive Types Supported by S2D

All-Flash

These can be combined in six ways, which Microsoft groups into two categories: "all-flash" and "hybrid".

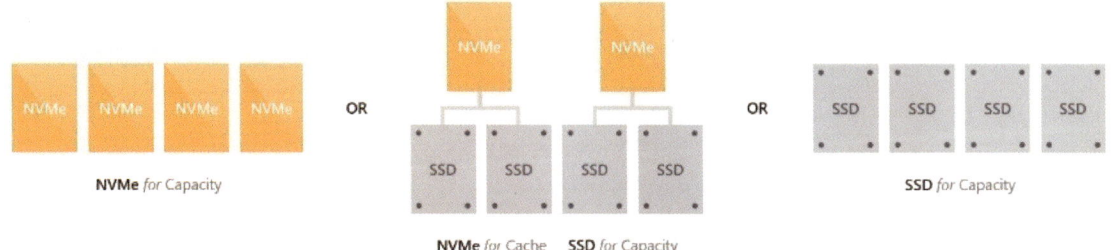

Figure 18 – All Flash Deployments

Hybrid

Hybrid deployments aim to balance performance and capacity or to maximize capacity and include rotational drives.

Figure 19 – Hybrid Deployments

Cache Drive Selection

In deployments with multiple types of drives, Storage Spaces Direct automatically uses all drives of the "fastest" type for caching. The remaining drives are used for capacity.

Which type is "fastest" is determined according to the following hierarchy.

Chapter 2   Introducing Storage Spaces Direct (S2D)

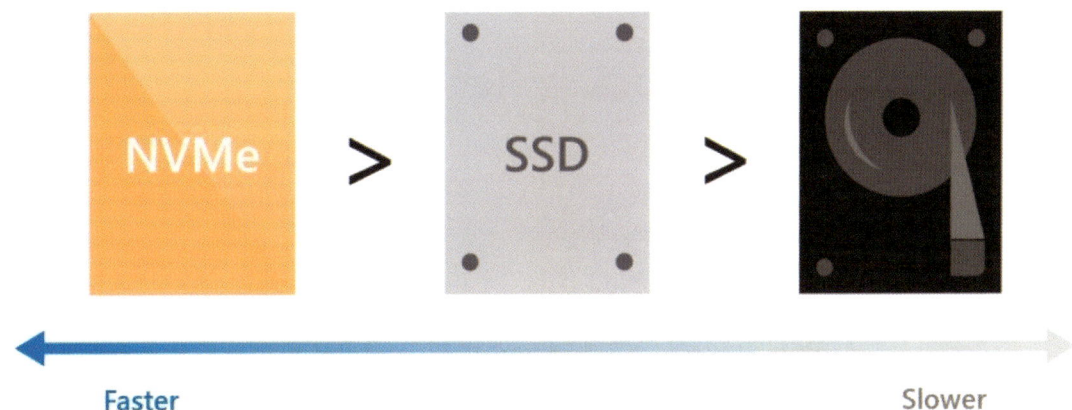

Figure 20 – Automatic Cache Drive Selection

For example, if you have NVMe and SSDs, the NVMe will cache for the SSDs.

If you have SSDs and HDDs, the SSDs will cache for the HDDs.

> **Note:** Cache drives do not contribute usable storage capacity. All data stored in the cache is also stored elsewhere, or will be once it de-stages. This means that your total raw storage capacity equals the sum of your capacity drives only.

When all drives are of the same type, no cache is configured automatically. You have the option to manually configure higher-endurance drives to cache for lower-endurance drives of the same type.

In all-NVMe or all-SSD deployments, especially at very small scale, having no drives "spent" on cache can improve storage efficiency meaningfully.

Cache behavior

Your cache's behavior is determined automatically, depending on the type(s) of drives that are being cached for. For example, if SSD is used to cache for hard disk drives, both reads and writes will be cached. If using NVMe to cache for SSD drives, only writes are cached.

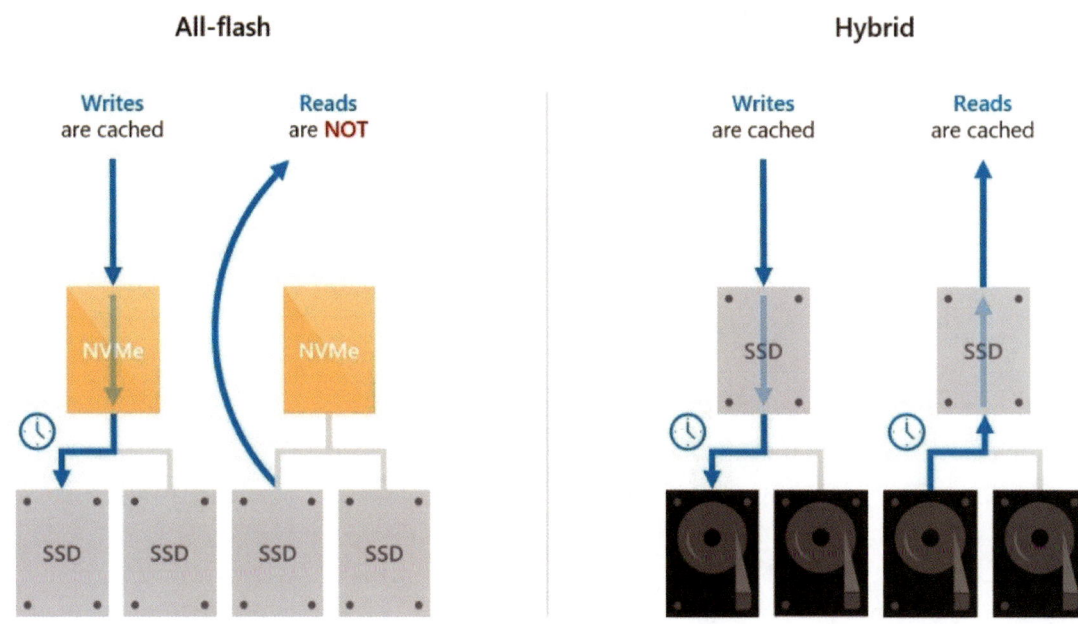

Figure 21 – Cache Behavior

Write-only caching for all-flash deployments

When caching for solid-state drives (NVMe or SSDs), only writes are cached. Because writes and rewrites often coalesce in the cache and de-stage only as needed, this reduces wear on the capacity drives. The cumulative traffic to the capacity drives is reduced, extending their lifetime. For this reason your cache drives should be higher endurance, write optimized drives. Your capacity drives can perform adequately with lower write endurance.

Solid-state drives universally offer low read latency, and reads do not significantly affect the lifespan of flash drives. Because of this, reads are not cached. Instead, they are served directly from the capacity drives. For solid-state only deployments, this allows the cache to be dedicated exclusively to writes, maximizing efficiency.

In an all SSD deployment, therefore, write characteristics are determined by the cache drive, while read characteristics are dictated by the capacity drives. This ensures a consistent, predictable and uniform experience for both.

Read/write caching for hybrid deployments

In a hybrid deployment, the SSD based cache is used to cache both reads and writes, in order to provide flash-like latency (often ~10x better) for both reads and writes. Frequently or recently accessed read data is stored for fast access, and to minimize random traffic to the hard disk drives (random access to HDDs can result in considerable latency and lost time, due to seek and rotational delays). As with all-flash deployments, writes and rewrites coalesce in the cache. The cache is used to minimize the cumulative traffic to the capacity drives, and to absorb bursts. To improve performance even further, Storage Spaces Direct implements an algorithm that de-randomizes writes before de-staging them. By doing so, S2D emulates an IO pattern to disk to make it seem sequential even when the actual IO coming from the workload (such as virtual machines) is random. This maximizes the IOPS and throughput to the HDDs.

Caching in deployments with drives of all three types

When drives of all three types are present, the NVMe drives provide caching for both the SSDs and the HDDs. As described above, only writes are cached for the SSDs, and both reads and writes are cached for the HDDs. The burden of caching for the HDDs is distributed evenly among the cache drives.

Deployment	Cache Drives	Capacity Drives	Cache behavior (default)
All NVMe	None	NVMe	Write-only (if configured)
All SSD	None	SSD	Write-only (if configured)
NVMe + SSD	NVMe	SSD	Write-Only
NVMe + HDD	NVMe	HDD	Read + Write
SSD + HDD	SSD	HDD	Read + Write
NVMe + SSD + HDD	NVMe	SSD + HDD	Rad + Write for HDD, Write-only for SSD

Cache Architecture

In S2D, cache is implemented at the drive level. This means that cache drives within one server are bound to one or many of the capacity drives within the same server.

Because the cache is below the rest of the software-defined storage stack, it does not have nor need any awareness of concepts such as Storage Spaces or fault tolerance. You can think of it as creating "hybrid" (e.g. part flash, part disk) drives which are then presented to Windows. Much like an actual hybrid drive, the transition of hot and cold data between faster and slower portions of the storage is all but invisible from the outside.

As we previously established that resiliency in storage spaces is at least server-level, (data copies are always written to a separate server or servers; at most one copy per server), cached data is automatically afforded the same resiliency as data not in the cache.

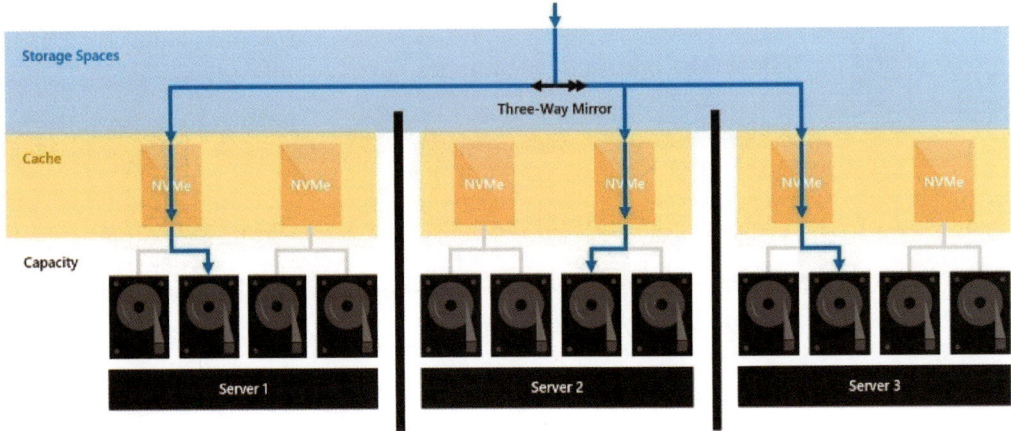

Figure 22 – Server Side Cache Architecture

For example, when using three-way mirroring, three copies of any data are written to different servers, where they land in cache. Regardless of whether they are later de-staged or not, three copies will always exist.

Drive bindings are dynamic

Cache bindings can be set to any ratio you want, from 1:1 to 1:12, or beyond. Once the ratio is set, it will adjust automatically whenever drives are added or removed, whether scaling up, or after a failure. This allows you to add capacity drives or cache drives whenever you want, without repercussions.

As best practice, we recommend that the number of capacity drives be a multiple of the number of cache drives, to ensure even and predictable performance. If you have 4 cache drives for example, you will experience more even and predictable performance with 8 capacity drives than you would with 7 or 9.

Handling cache drive failures

If a cache drive fails, any write data that has not yet been de-staged is lost to the local server. However, the data remains as copies in the other servers. As with any other drive failure, Storage Spaces will recover the data automatically by consulting the surviving copies.

If such a failure occurs, the capacity drives bound to the lost cache drive will appear unhealthy. For a brief period, the capacity drives which were bound to the lost cache drive will appear unhealthy. This state is temporary, and will resume showing healthy ad soon as cache rebinding has occurred. It is for this reason that a minimum of two cache drives are required per server.

Relationship to other caches

The Windows software-defined storage stack contains a number of other unrelated caches. These include, (but are not limited to): the Storage Spaces write-back cache, the ReFS read cache, and the Cluster Shared Volume (CSV) in-memory read cache.There are several other unrelated caches in the Windows software-defined storage stack. Examples include the Storage Spaces write-back cache, the ReFS read cache, and the Cluster Shared Volume (CSV) in-memory read cache.

Neither the Storage Spaces write-back cache, nor the ReFS read cache should be modified from their default behavior in S2D. Parameters such as **-WriteCacheSize** on the **New-Volume** cmdlet, for example, should <u>not</u> be used.

The CSV cache can provide valuable performance gains in certain scenarios. It is entirely optional. By default, it is off in Storage Spaces Direct, but it does not conflict in any way with the new cache described in this topic.

Manual Cache configuration

Cache cannot be and is not configured automatically in deployments where all drives are of the same type, such as all-NVMe or all-SSD deployments. This is because Windows cannot distinguish characteristics like write endurance automatically among drives of the same type.

While cache will not be configured automatically, you can still manually create a cache using higher-endurance drives to cache for lower-endurance drives of the same type. To do so, you will specify which drive model to use with the -CacheDeviceModel parameter of the Enable-ClusterS2D cmdlet. Once Storage Spaces Direct is enabled, all drives of that model will be used for caching.

```
PS C:\> Get-PhysicalDisk | Group Model -NoElement

Count Name
----- ----
    8 FABRIKAM NVME-1710
   16 CONTOSO NVME-1520

PS C:\> Enable-ClusterS2D -CacheDeviceModel "FABRIKAM NVME-1710"
```

To verify that the selected drives are being used for caching, you can run the Get-PhysicalDisk cmdlet in PowerShell and verify that their Usage property says "Journal".

Set cache behavior

It is possible to override the default behavior of the cache. For example, you can set it to cache reads even in an all-flash deployment. Microsoft discourages modifying the behavior unless you are certain the default does not suit your workload.

To override the behavior, use Set-ClusterS2D cmdlet and its **-CacheModeSSD** and **-CacheModeHDD** parameters. The **CacheModeSSD** parameter sets the cache behavior when caching for solid-state drives. The **CacheModeHDD** parameter sets cache behavior when caching for hard disk drives. This can be done at any time after Storage Spaces Direct is enabled.

You can use **Get-ClusterS2D** to verify the behavior is set.

Chapter 2   Introducing Storage Spaces Direct (S2D)

```
PS C:\> Get-ClusterS2D

CacheModeHDD : ReadWrite
CacheModeSSD : WriteOnly
...

PS C:\> Set-ClusterS2D -CacheModeSSD ReadWrite

PS C:\> Get-ClusterS2D
```

Sizing the cache

The cache should be sized to accommodate the working set (the data being actively read or written at any given time) of your applications and workloads.

This is especially important in hybrid deployments with hard disk drives. If the active working set exceeds the size of the cache, or if the active working set drifts too quickly, read cache misses will increase and writes will need to be de-staged more aggressively, hurting overall performance.

You can use the built-in Performance Monitor (PerfMon.exe) utility in Windows to inspect the rate of cache misses. Specifically, you can compare the Cache Miss Reads/sec from the Cluster Storage Hybrid Disk counter set to the overall read IOPS of your deployment. Each "Hybrid Disk" corresponds to one capacity drive.

For example, 2 cache drives bound to 4 capacity drives results in 4 "Hybrid Disk" object instances per server.

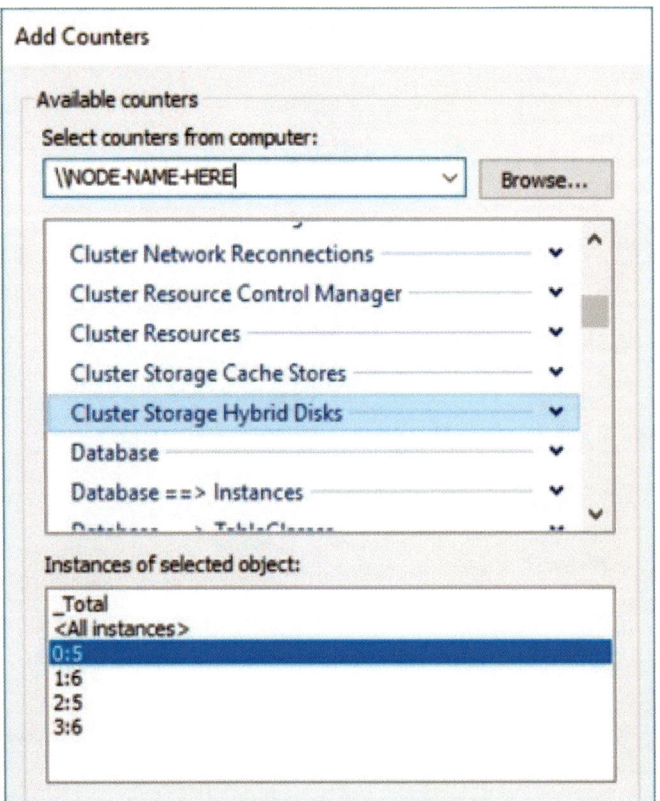

Figure 25 – Cache Performance Counters

Chapter 2 Introducing Storage Spaces Direct (S2D)

Chapter 3

Windows Server 2016 Failover Clustering

Failover clustering - a Windows Server feature that enables you to group multiple servers together into a fault-tolerant cluster - provides new and improved features for software-defined datacenter customers and many other workloads running clusters on physical hardware or in virtual machines.

Independent servers and computers can fail for any number of reasons, and it is rarely, if ever, a desirable outcome. A failover cluster groups together independent machines to work together to to ensure that data or applications remain functional even should such a failure occur. Connected by physical cables and software, each server can leverage the resources of their clustered counterparts to ensure continuity. Each clustered server (or sometimes group of servers) is called a node. If one or more of the cluster nodes fail, other nodes begin to provide service (a process known as failover). In addition, the clustered roles are proactively monitored to verify that they are working properly. If they are not working, they are restarted or moved to another node.

Failover clusters also provide Cluster Shared Volume (CSV) functionality that provides a consistent, distributed namespace that clustered roles can use to access shared storage from all nodes. With the Failover Clustering feature, users experience a minimum of disruptions in service.

Failover Clustering has many practical applications, including:

- Highly available or continuously available file share storage for applications such as Microsoft SQL Server and Hyper-V virtual machines
- Highly available clustered roles that run on physical servers or on virtual machines that are installed on servers running Hyper-V
- Primary interface for configuring S2D

What's new for Windows Server 2016

In the following section, we will share with you some of the new features in Windows Server 2016. The below descriptions are a high level overview.

Chapter 3   Windows Server 2016 Failover Clustering

Cluster operating system rolling upgrades

In Windows Server 2016, a new feature enables an administrator to upgrade the operating system of the cluster nodes from Windows Server 2012 R2 to the new OS without stopping Hyper-V or the Scale-Out File Server workloads. This feature, called the Cluster Operating System Rolling Upgrade, allows your organization to avoid the downtime penalties usually incurred against your Service Level Agreement (SLA) by the upgrade process.

To keep the cluster's services running, and prevent downtime, the cluster will continue to function at a Windows Server 2012 R2 level until all of the nodes in the cluster are running Windows Server 2016. The cluster functional level is upgraded to Windows Server 2016 by using the Windows PowerShell cmdlt **Update-ClusterFunctionalLevel.**

> **Note:** After the cluster functional level is updated, you cannot go back to a Windows Server 2012 R2 cluster functional level.
>
> Until the Update-ClusterFunctionalLevel cmdlet is run, the process is reversible, and Windows Server 2012 R2 nodes can be added and Windows Server 2016 nodes can be removed.

A Hyper-V or Scale-Out File Server failover cluster can now easily be upgraded without any downtime, and without the need to build a new cluster with nodes running the Windows Server 2016 operating system. Migrating to Windows Server 2012 R2 was a much more involved task, requiring that the existing cluster be taken offline, and each node reinstalled with the new operating system, and then the cluster could be brought online. Obviously this was cumbersome, and required considerable downtime. The ability to keep your cluster online throughout your Windows Server 2016 upgrade is a big step forward.

The Cluster Operating System Rolling Upgrade feature performs the upgrade in phases. These phases are as follows for each node in a cluster:

1. The node is paused and drained of all virtual machines that are running on it.

2. The virtual machines (or other cluster workload) are migrated to another node in the cluster.The virtual machines are migrated to another node in the cluster.

3. The existing operating system is removed and a clean installation of the Windows Server 2016 operating system on the node is performed.

4. The node running the Windows Server 2016 operating system is added back to the cluster.

5. At this point, the cluster is said to be running in mixed mode, because the cluster nodes are running either Windows Server 2012 R2 or Windows Server 2016.

6. The cluster functional level stays at Windows Server 2012 R2. At this functional level, new features in Windows Server 2016 that affect compatibility with previous versions of the operating system will be unavailable.

7. Eventually, all nodes are upgraded to Windows Server 2016.
8. Finally, Cluster functional level is changed to Windows Server 2016 using the Windows PowerShell cmdlet Update-ClusterFunctionalLevel. At this point, you can take advantage of the Windows Server 2016 features.

Rolling cluster upgrades are an extremely important new feature of Windows 2016 in relation to S2D. It is very likely that when the next version of Windows Server 2016 "R2" comes out we will likely be able to upgrade our S2D nodes on the fly with little to no downtime.

Storage Replica

Another new feature in Windows Server 2016 is Storage Replica. This new feature enables storage-agnostic, block-level, synchronous replication between servers or clusters for disaster recovery, as well as the ability to stretch a failover cluster between sites. Synchronous replication enables mirroring of data in physical sites with crash-consistent volumes to ensure zero data loss at the file-system level. Asynchronous replication allows site extension beyond metropolitan ranges with the possibility of data loss.

Storage Replica enables you to do the following:

- Provide a single vendor disaster recovery solution for planned and unplanned outages of mission critical workloads.
- Use SMB3 transport with proven reliability, scalability, and performance.
- Stretch Windows failover clusters across metropolitan distances.
- Use Microsoft software end to end for storage and clustering, such as Hyper-V, Storage Replica, Storage Spaces, Cluster, Scale-Out File Server, SMB3, Data Deduplication, and ReFS/NTFS.

Storage Replica helps to reduce cost and complexity as follows:
- Is hardware agnostic, with no requirement for a specific storage configurations like DAS or SAN.
- Allows commodity storage and networking technologies.
- Features ease of graphical management for individual nodes and clusters through Failover Cluster Manager.
- Includes comprehensive, large-scale scripting options through Windows PowerShell.

- Helps reduce downtime, and increase reliability and productivity intrinsic to Windows.
- Provides supportability, performance metrics, and diagnostic capabilities.

Cloud Witness for a Failover Cluster

Windows Server 2016 also enhances standard quorum witness functionality, by extending it to the cloud. Cloud Witness is a new type of Failover Cluster quorum witness that leverages Microsoft Azure as the arbitration point. The Cloud Witness, like any other quorum witness, gets a vote and can participate in the quorum calculations. You can configure cloud witness as a quorum witness using the Configure a Cluster Quorum Wizard.

What value does this change add?

Using Cloud Witness as a Failover Cluster quorum witness provides the following advantages:

- Leverages Microsoft Azure and eliminates the need for a third separate datacenter.
- Uses the standard publicly available Microsoft Azure Blob Storage which eliminates the extra maintenance overhead of VMs hosted in a public cloud.
- The same Microsoft Azure Storage Account can be used for multiple clusters (one blob file per cluster; cluster unique id used as blob file name).
- Provides a very low on-going cost to the Storage Account (a very small amount of data written per blob file, with the blob file updated only once when cluster nodes' state changes).

Fault Domains

Failover Clustering enables multiple servers to work together to provide high availability – or put another way, to provide node fault tolerance. But today's businesses demand ever-greater availability from their infrastructure. To achieve cloud-like uptime, even highly unlikely occurrences such as chassis failures, rack outages, or natural disasters must be protected against. That's why Failover Clustering in Windows Server 2016 introduces chassis, rack, and site fault tolerance as well.

Fault domains and fault tolerance are closely related concepts. A fault domain is a set of hardware components that share a single point of failure. To be fault tolerant to a certain level, you need multiple fault domains at that level. For example, to be rack fault tolerant, your servers and your data must be distributed across multiple racks.

- **Storage Spaces, including S2D, uses fault domains to maximize data safety.**

  Resiliency in Storage Spaces is conceptually like distributed, software-defined RAID. Multiple copies of all data are kept in sync, ensuring that if hardware fails and one copy is lost, others are recopied to restore resiliency. To achieve the best possible resiliency, copies should be kept in separate fault domains.

- **The Health Service uses fault domains to provide more helpful alerts.**

  Each fault domain can be associated with location metadata, which will automatically be included in any subsequent alerts. These descriptors can assist operations or maintenance personnel and reduce errors by disambiguating hardware.

  Stretch clustering uses fault domains for storage affinity.
  Stretch clustering allows faraway servers to join a common cluster. For the best performance, applications or virtual machines should be run on servers that are nearby to those providing their storage. Fault domain awareness enables this storage affinity.

Levels of fault domains

There are four canonical levels of fault domains - site, rack, chassis, and node. Nodes are discovered automatically; each additional level is optional. For example, if your deployment does not use blade servers, the chassis level may not make sense for you.

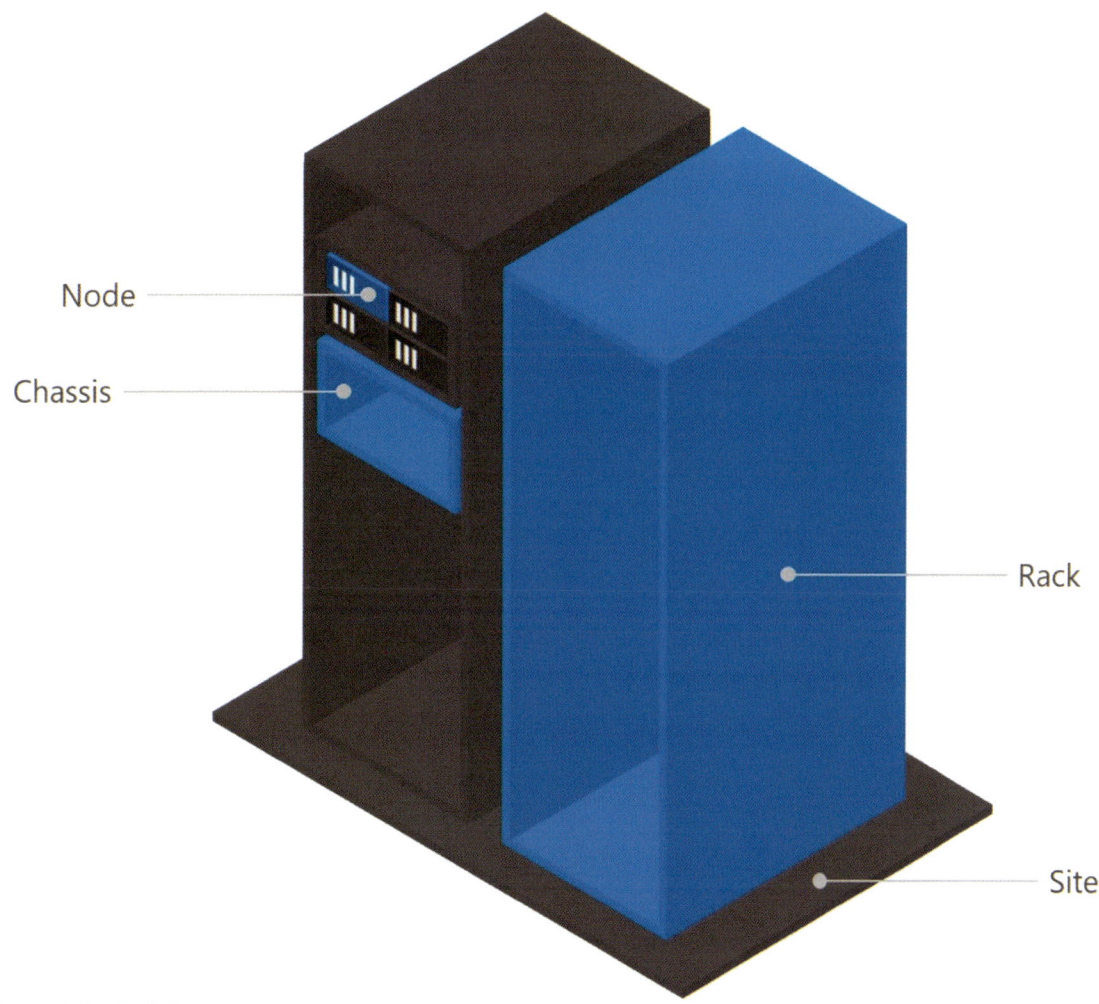

Figure 26 – Fault Domains

Configuring Cluster Fault Domains

This example would use the following XML file to configure Two Sites, and one rack in each site.

```xml
<Topology>
  <Site Name="SEA" Location="Contoso HQ, 123 Example St, Room 4010, Seattle">
    <Rack Name="A01" Location="Aisle A, Rack 01">
      <Node Name="Server01" Location="Rack Unit 33" />
      <Node Name="Server02" Location="Rack Unit 35" />
      <Node Name="Server03" Location="Rack Unit 37" />
    </Rack>
  </Site>
  <Site Name="NYC" Location="Regional Datacenter, 456 Example Ave, New York City">
    <Rack Name="B07" Location="Aisle B, Rack 07">
      <Node Name="Server04" Location="Rack Unit 20" />
      <Node Name="Server05" Location="Rack Unit 22" />
      <Node Name="Server06" Location="Rack Unit 24" />
    </Rack>
  </Site>
</Topology>
```

To apply the configuration of the Fault Domains you would run the following PowerShell command.

```
$xml = Get-Content <Path> | Out-String
Set-ClusterFaultDomainXML -XML $xml
```

Virtual Machine Resiliency

Windows Server 2016 includes increased virtual machines compute resiliency to help reduce intra-cluster communication issues in your compute cluster as follows:

- **Resiliency options available for virtual machines:** You can now configure virtual machine resiliency options that define behavior of the virtual machines during transient failures:

  - Resiliency Level: Helps you define how the transient failures are handled.

  - Resiliency Period: Helps you define how long all the virtual machines are allowed to run isolated.

- **Quarantine of unhealthy nodes:** Unhealthy nodes are quarantined and are no longer allowed to join the cluster. This prevents flapping nodes from negatively effecting other nodes and the overall cluster.

With Storage Resiliency in Windows Server 2016, virtual machines are more resilient to transient storage failures. The improved virtual machine resiliency helps preserve tenant virtual machine session states in the event of a storage disruption. Quick and intelligent virtual machine response to storage infrastructure issues ensures this.

The process by which storage resiliency and compute resiliency restore a VM's session state goes something like this:

When a virtual machine disconnects from its underlying storage, it pauses and waits for storage to recover. While paused, the virtual machine retains the context of applications that are running in it. When the virtual machine's connection to its storage is restored, the virtual machine returns to its running state. As a result, the tenant machine's session state is retained on recovery.

Site-aware Failover Clusters

Windows Server 2016 includes site- aware failover clusters that enable group nodes in stretched clusters based on their physical location (site). Cluster site-awareness enhances key operations during the cluster lifecycle such as failover behavior, placement policies, heartbeat between the nodes, and quorum behavior.

Workgroup and Multi-domain clusters

In Windows Server 2012 R2 and previous versions, a cluster can only be created between member nodes joined to the same domain. Windows Server 2016 breaks down these barriers and introduces the ability to create a Failover Cluster without Active Directory dependencies. You can now create failover clusters in the following configurations:

- **Single-domain Clusters.** Clusters with all nodes joined to the same domain.
- **Multi-domain Clusters.** Clusters with nodes which are members of different domains.
- **Workgroup Clusters.** Clusters with nodes which are member servers / workgroup (not domain joined).

VM load balancing

Virtual machine Load Balancing is a new feature in Failover Clustering that facilitates the seamless load balancing of virtual machines across the nodes in a cluster. Over-committed nodes are identified based on virtual machine Memory and CPU utilization on the node. Virtual machines are then moved (live migrated) from an over-committed node to nodes with available bandwidth (if applicable). The aggressiveness of the balancing can be tuned to ensure optimal cluster performance and utilization. Load Balancing is enabled by default in Windows Sever 2016 Technical Preview. However, Load Balancing is disabled when SCVMM Dynamic Optimization is enabled.

Virtual Machine Start Order

Virtual machine Start Order is a new feature in Failover Clustering that introduces start order orchestration for Virtual machines (and all groups) in a cluster. Virtual machines can now be grouped into tiers, and start order dependencies can be created between different tiers. This ensures that the most important virtual machines (such as Domain Controllers or Utility virtual machines) are started first. Virtual machines are not started until the virtual machines that they have a dependency on are also started.

Simplified SMB Multichannel and multi-NIC cluster networks

Failover Cluster networks are no longer limited to a single NIC per subnet / network. With Simplified SMB Multi-channel and Multi-NIC Cluster Networks, network configuration is automatic and every NIC on the subnet can be used for cluster and workload traffic. This enhancement allows customers to maximize network throughput for Hyper-V, SQL Server Failover Cluster Instance, and other SMB workloads. It also enables easier configuration of multiple network adapters in a cluster.

Diagnostic Improvements

When troubleshooting a S2D Cluster it is important to understand where and how to use its advanced logging and diagnostic capabilities. The section below will guide us on how to diagnose issues with failover clusters.

Windows Server 2016 includes the following new cluster diagnostic capabilities:

- **Cluster.Log** - Enhancements to Cluster log files (such as Time Zone Information and Diagnostic Verbose log) make it easier to troubleshoot failover clustering issues.
- **Active Memory Dump** - filters out most memory pages allocated to virtual machines, and therefore makes the memory.dmp file much smaller and easier to save or copy.

Cluster Log Enhancements

Here we will provide details about the improvements made in the tools and methods for troubleshooting Failover Clusters with Windows Server 2016.

Failover Cluster has diagnostic logs running on each server that allow in-depth troubleshooting of problems without having to reproduce the issue. This log is valuable for Microsoft's support as well as those out there who have expertise at troubleshooting failover clusters.

> **Helpful Hint:** Always go to the system event log first when troubleshooting an issue. Failover cluster posts events in the System event log that are often enough to understand the nature and scope of the problem. It also gives you the specific date/time of the problem, which is useful if you need to look at other event logs or dig into the cluster.log afterwards.

Generating the Cluster.log

This is not a new feature, but any discussion of cluster log enhancements is moot if you do not know how to obtain your logs. This is for the benefit of those that are not already familiar with generating the cluster log.

Get-ClusterLog is the Windows PowerShell cmdlet that will generate the cluster.log on each server that is a member of the cluster and is currently running. The output looks like this on a 3-node cluster:

Chapter 3   Windows Server 2016 Failover Clustering

```
PS C:\Windows\system32> get-clusterlog

Mode                LastWriteTime         Length Name
----                -------------         ------ ----
-a----        4/29/2015   11:43 AM       66071616 Cluster.log
-a----        4/29/2015   11:43 AM       56876386 Cluster.log
-a----        4/29/2015   11:44 AM       74238390 Cluster.log

PS C:\Windows\system32>
```

Figure 25 – Get-Clusterlog

The Cluster.log files can be found in the **<systemroot>\cluster\reports** directory (usually c:\windows\cluster\Reports) on each node.

The **–Destination** parameter can be used to cause the files to be copied to a specified directory with the Server's name appended to the log name, which makes it much easier to get and analyze logs from multiple servers:

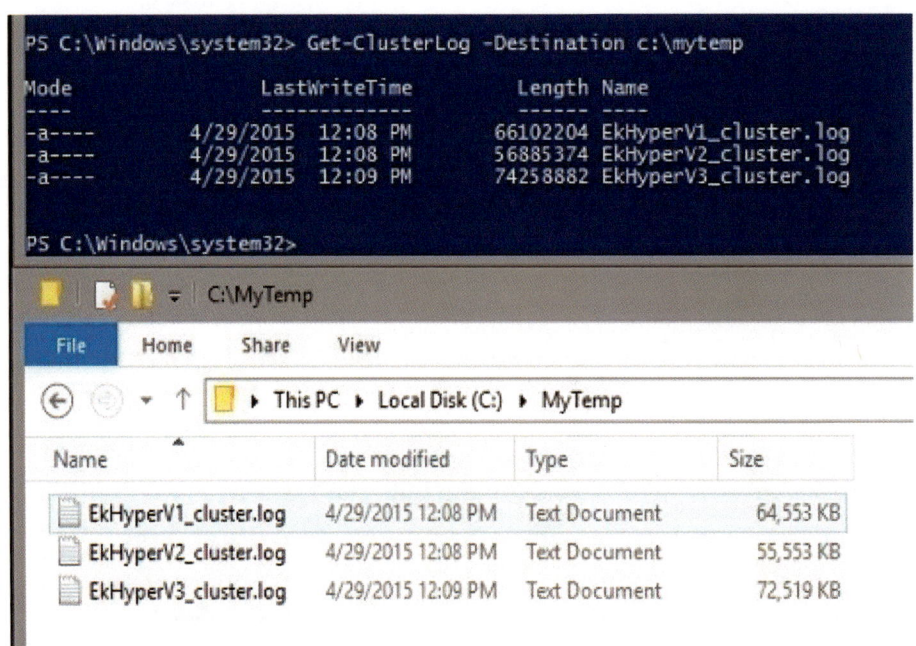

Figure 27 – Changing the location of Cluster.log

What's New in Windows Server 2016

The improvements to Windows Server 2016 Failover Cluster Diagnostic logging are important to understand when troubleshooting a failed S2D Cluster. The following section outlines these improvements at a high level.

TimeZone Information

The cluster.log is a large dump of information from the system, captured in a text file. The time stamps default to UTC (which some people call GMT). This means that you must determine the time zone you are in, and add or subtract hours from the stated time in the time stamp accordingly. For example, if your time zone is UTC +8 you would add 8 hours to the time stamp listed for the event in your log. If it was UTC – 8, you would subtract 8 hours.

Microsoft offers 2 enhancements in the **cluster.log** that makes this time zone and UTC offset easier to discover and work with:

UTC offset of the server noted: At the top of the cluster.log notes it now states the UTC offset of the originating server. In the example below, it notes that the server is set to UTC, with a plus 7 hour offset added (420 minutes).

Specifically noting this offset in the log removes the guesswork related to the system's time zone setting.

Cluster log can be set to use UTC or local time: The top of the cluster.log also notes whether the log was created using UTC or local time for the timestamps. The –**UseLocalTime** parameter for **Get-ClusterLog** causes the cluster.log to write timestamps that are already adjusted for the server's time zone instead of using UTC. The feature itself is not new, but it became obvious that it was important to know whether the parameter was used or not, so it is now noted in the log.

```
[===Cluster ===]
```

UTC= localtime + time zone offset; with daylight savings, the time zone offset of this machine is 420 minutes, or 7 hours

The logs were generated using Coordinated Universal Time (UTC). 'Get-ClusterLog - UseLocalTime' will generate in local time.

> **Note:** The sections of the cluster.log are encased in [=== ===], which makes it easy to navigate down the log to each section by doing a find on "[===". As a bit of trivia, this format was chosen because it looks a little like a Tie Fighter and Microsoft thought it looked cool.

Cluster Objects

Every cluster has 'objects' that are part of its configuration. Getting the details of these objects can be useful in diagnosing problems. These objects include resources, groups, resource types, nodes, networks, network interfaces, and volumes. The cluster.log now dumps these objects in a Comma Separated Values list with headers.

Here is an example:

```
[===Networks ===]

Name,Id,description,role,transport,ignore,AssociatedInterfaces,PrefixList
,address,addressMask,ipV6Address,state,linkSpeed,rdmaCapable,rssCapable,a
utoMetric,metric,

Cluster Network 1,27f2d19b-7e23-4ee3-a226-
287d4ebe9113,,1,TCP/IP,false,82e5107c-5375-473a-ab9f-
5b6450bf5c7f30ff5ff6-00a3-494b-84b6-62a27ef99bb3 187c582d-f23c-48f4-8c37-
6a452b2a238b,10.10.1.0/24
,10.10.1.0,255.255.255.0,,3,1000000000,false,false,true,39984,

Cluster Network 2,e6efd1f6-474b-410a-bd7b-
5ece99476cd8,,1,TCP/IP,false,57d9b74d-8d9e-4afe-8667-
e91e0bd23412617bb075-3803-4e5e-a039-db513d60603d 51c4fd42-9cb4-4f2e-a65c-
01fea9bfa582,10.10.3.0/24
,10.10.3.0,255.255.255.0,,3,1000000000,false,false,true,39985,

Cluster Network 3,1a5029c7-7961-40bb-b6b9-
dcbbe4187034,,3,TCP/IP,false,d3cdef35-82bc-4a60-8ed4-
5c2b278f7c0e83c7c4b8-b588-425c-bfae-0c69d7a45bcd c1fb12d2-071b-4cb2-8ca7-
fa04e972cd1c,157.59.132.0/22
2001:4898:28:4::/64,157.59.132.0,255.255.252.0,2001:4898:28:4::,3,1000000
00,false,false,true,80000,
```

These sections can be consumed by any application that can parse CSV text. Or, you can copy/paste into an Excel spreadsheet, which makes it easier to read as well as providing filter/sort/search functionality. For the example below, I pasted the above section into a spreadsheet and then used the "Text to Columns" action in the "DATA" tab of Microsoft's Excel.

	A	B	C	D	E	F	G	H	I	J	K	L	M	N	O	P	Q
1	[=== Networks ===]																
2	Name	Id	descriptio	role	transport	ignore	Associate	PrefixList	address	addressM	ipV6Addr	state	linkSpeed	rdmaCapa	rssCapabl	autoMetri	metric
3	Cluster Network 1	27f2d19b-7e23-4ee3-a226		1	TCP/IP	FALSE	82e5107c-	10.10.1.0/24	10.10.1.0	255.255.255.0		3	1000000000	FALSE	FALSE	TRUE	39984
4	Cluster Network 2	e6efd1f6-474b-410a-bd7b		1	TCP/IP	FALSE	57d9b74d	10.10.3.0/24	10.10.3.0	255.255.255.0		3	1000000000	FALSE	FALSE	TRUE	39985
5	Cluster Network 3	1a5029c7-7961-40bb-b6b9		3	TCP/IP	FALSE	d3cdef35-	157.xx.xx.0/2	157.xx.xx.	255.255.25	2001:4898	3	100000000	FALSE	FALSE	TRUE	80000
6																	

Figure 28 – Viewing Cluster.log sections in Excel

Diagnostic Verbose Logging

New in Windows Server 2016 is the **Diagnostic Verbose** event channel. This is a new channel that is in addition to the Diagnostic channel for **FailoverClustering.**

In most cases the diagnostic channel, with the default log level set to the default of 3, gets enough information that an expert troubleshooter or Microsoft's support engineers can understand a problem. However, there are occasions where we need more verbose logging and it is necessary to set the cluster log level to 5, causing the diagnostic channel to start adding the verbose level of events to the log. After changing the log level, you must then reproduce the problem and analyze the logs again.

The question arises, why is it not best practice to keep the log level at 5? The answer is that this causes the logs to have more events and therefore wrap faster. The ability to go back for hours or days in the logs is often necessary as well, so the quicker wrapping can pose its own troubleshooting problem.

To accommodate wanting verbose logging for the most recent time-frame, and having logging that provides adequate history, a parallel diagnostic channel called DiagnosticVerbose was implemented. The DiagnosticVerbose log is always set for the equivalent of the cluster log level 5 (verbose) and runs in parallel to the Diagnostic channel for FailoverClustering.

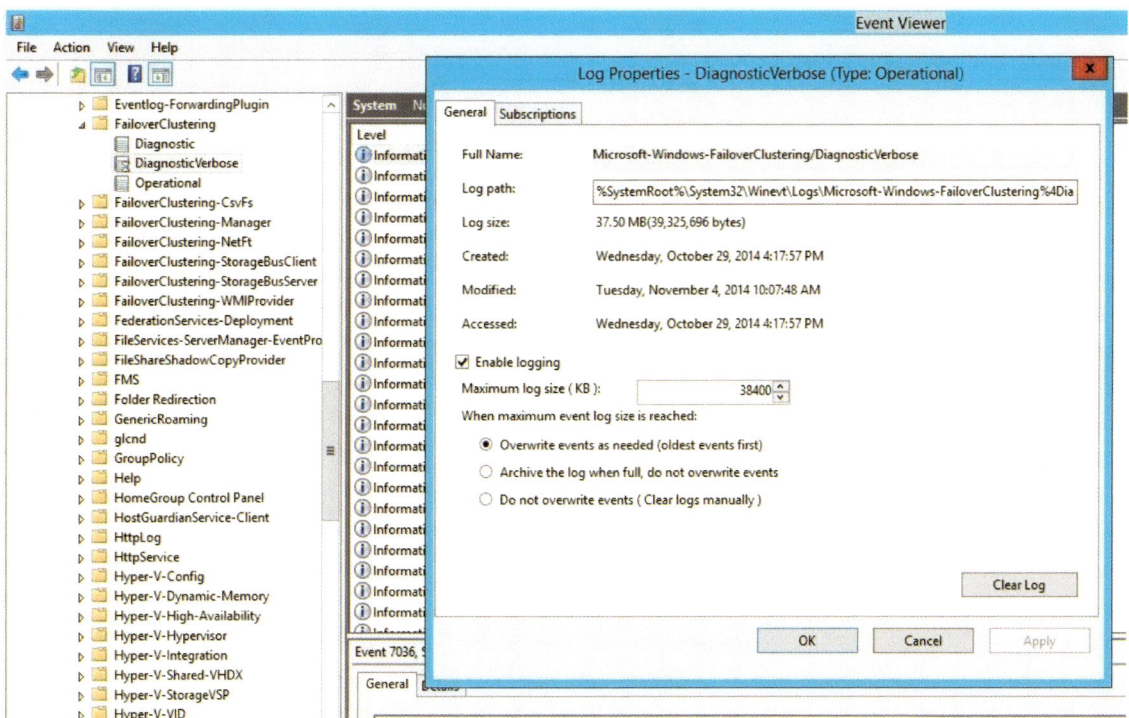
Figure 29 – Diagnostic Verbose Logging

You can find the DiagnosticVerbose section in the cluster.log by doing a find (Ctrl +f) on "DiagnosticVerbose". Find will take you to the section header:

```
[=== Microsoft-Windows-FailoverClustering/DiagnosticVerbose ===]

[Verbose] 00000244.00001644::2015/04/22-01:04:29.623 DBG
[RCM] rcm::PreemptionTracker::GetPreemptedGroups()
[Verbose] 00000244.00001644::2015/04/22-01:04:29.623 DBG
[RCM] got asked for preempted groups, returning 0 records
```

The Diagnostic channel (default log level of 3) can be found by doing a find on "Cluster Logs":

```
[=== Cluster Logs ===]

00000e68.00000cfc::2015/03/23-22:12:24.682 DBG    [NETFTAPI] received
NsiInitialNotification
00000e68.00000cfc::2015/03/23-22:12:24.684 DBG    [NETFTAPI] received
NsiInitialNotification
```

Events from Other Channels

One of the tips noted above states the recommendation to start in the system event log first. However, it is not uncommon for someone to generate the cluster logs and send them to their internal 3rd tier support or to other experts. Going back and getting the system or other event logs that may be useful in diagnosing the problem can take time, and sometimes the logs have already wrapped or have been cleared.

In Windows Server 2016 cluster log, the following event channels are now also dumped into the cluster.log for each node. Since they are all in one file, you no longer need to go to the nodes and pull each log individually, saving you time in a troubleshooting scenario.

```
[=== System ===]

[=== Microsoft-Windows-FailoverClustering/Operational logs ===]

[=== Microsoft-Windows-ClusterAwareUpdating-Management/Admin logs ===]

[=== Microsoft-Windows-ClusterAwareUpdating/Admin logs ===]
```

An example of this would look like this:

```
[=== System ===]

[System]
00000244.00001b3c::2015/03/24-19:46:34.671 ERR
Cluster resource 'Virtual Machine <name>' of type 'Virtual
```

```
Machine' in clustered role '<name>' failed.
```

Based on the failure policies for the resource and role, the cluster service may try to bring the resource online on this node or move the group to another node of the cluster and then restart it. Check the resource and group state using Failover Cluster Manager or the **Get-ClusterResource** Windows PowerShell cmdlet.

```
[System] 00000244.000016dc::2015/04/14-23:43:09.458 INFO The Cluster
service has changed the password of account 'CLIUSR' on node '<node
name>'.
```

> **Note:** If the size of the cluster.log file is bigger than you desire, the –TimeSpan switch for Get-ClusterLog will limit how far back (in minutes) it will go back in time for the events. For instance, Get-Clusterlog –TimeSpan 10 will cause the cluster.log on each node to be created and only include events from the last 10 minutes. That includes the Diagnostic, DiagnosticVerbose, and other channels that are included in the report.

Active Memory Dump

Servers that are used as Hyper-V hosts tend to have a significant amount of RAM and a complete memory dump includes processor state as well as a dump of what is in RAM. This results in the potential for the dmp file for a Full Dump to be extremely large. On these Hyper-V hosts, the parent partition is usually a small percentage of the overall RAM of the system, with the majority of the RAM allocated to Virtual Machines(VMs). It is the parent partition memory that is interesting in debugging a bugcheck or other bluescreen and the VM memory pages are typically not important for diagnosing most problems.

Windows Server 2016 introduces a dump type of "Active memory dump", which filters out most memory pages allocated to VMs and therefore makes the memory.dmp much smaller and easier to save/copy.

> **Note:** Now that we are building a hyper-converged solution with S2D it is imperative that we look at using the Active Memory Dump feature because the hosts will have 256 GB+ RAM on average in this configuration.

To illustrate the difference in file size obtained via a complete dump, as opposed to an Active Memory dump, we initiated bluescreens with different crash dump settings on a 16 GB system running Hyper-V. The results can be seen below. The first test was a complete memory dump, to provide a baseline. As you can see, this baseline roughly corresponds with the full amount of RAM in the system. This shows that a complete dump on a production Hyper-V system with hundreds of gigabytes of RAM is just not the best option.

The second test was to initiate a crash and perform an Active Memory Dump on the same system, with no VMs running. This resulted in a memory.dmp file that was only 10% of the first.

The third test run was an Active Memory Dump of a crash with two VMs running, to show that the Active Memory Dump truly is ignoring VM memory events. As you can see, again we have a result approximately 10 percent of the size of the complete dump, proving that it indeed is largely ignoring the VM results.

	Memory.dmp in KB	% Compared to Complete
Complete Dump	16,683,673	
Active Dump (no VMs)	1,586,496	10 %
Active Dump (VMs with 8 GB RAM total)	1,629,497	10 %
Kernel Dump (VMs with 8 GB RAM total)	582,261	3%
Automatic Dump (VMs with 8GB RAM total)	587,941	4%

Note: The size of the Active Dump as compared to a complete dump will vary depending on the total host memory and what is running on the system.

In looking at the numbers in the table above, keep in mind that the Active Dump is larger than the kernel, but includes the usermode space of the parent partition, while being 10% of the size of the complete dump that would have normally been required to get the usermode space.

Configuring Active Memory Dump

To configure an Active Memory Dump, the new dump type can be chosen through the Startup and Recovery dialog as shown below:

Chapter 3 Windows Server 2016 Failover Clustering

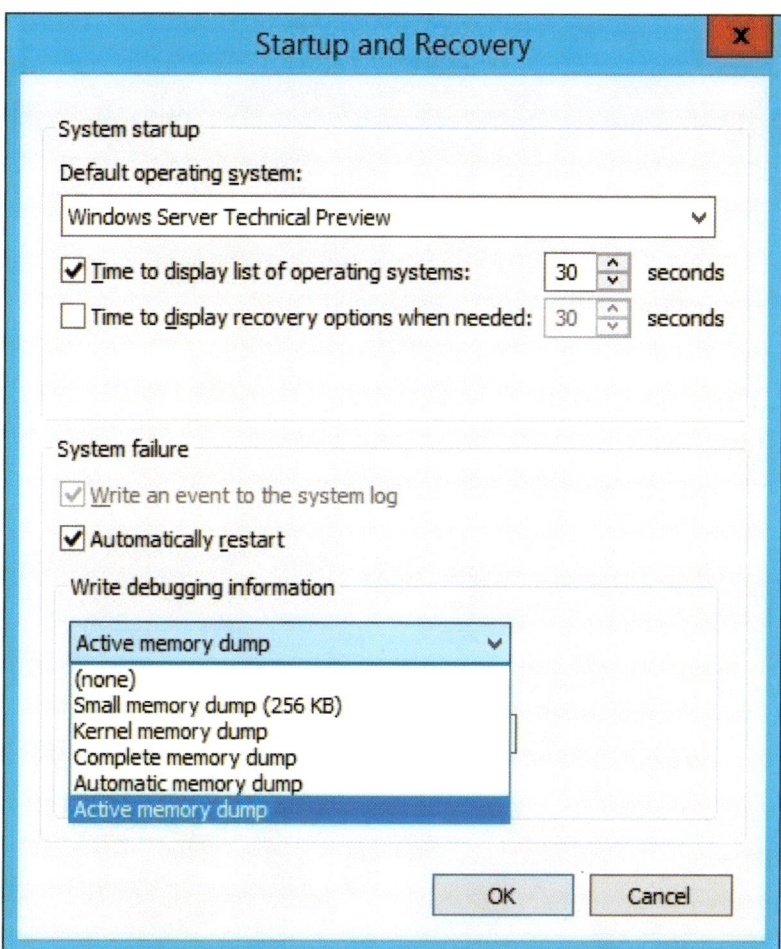

Figure 30 – Active Memory Dump

The memory.dmp type can also be set through the registry under the following key. The change will not take effect until the system is restarted if changing it directly in the registry:

```
HKEY_LOCAL_MACHINE\System\CurrentControlSet\Control\CrashControl\
```

To configure the Active memory.dmp there are 2 values that need to be set, both are REG_DWORD values.

```
HKEY_LOCAL_MACHINE\System\CurrentControlSet\Control\CrashControl\CrashDumpEnabled
```

The **CrashDumpEnabled** value needs to be 1, which is the same as a complete dump.

```
HKEY_LOCAL_MACHINE\System\CurrentControlSet\Control\CrashControl\FilterPa
ges.
```

The **FilterPages** value needs to be set to 1.

> **Note**: FilterPages value will not found under the
> HKEY_LOCAL_MACHINE\System\CurrentControlSet\Control\CrashControl\ key unless the
> GUI "Startup and Recovery" dialog is used to set the dump type to "Active Memory Dump", or
> unless you manually create and set the value.

The above can also be configured via PowerShell:

```
Get-ItemProperty -Path HKLM:\System\CurrentControlSet\Control\CrashControl -Name CrashDumpEnabled
Get-ItemProperty -Path HKLM:\System\CurrentControlSet\Control\CrashControl -Name FilterPages
Set-ItemProperty -Path HKLM:\System\CurrentControlSet\Control\CrashControl -Name CrashDumpEnabled -value 1
Set-ItemProperty -Path HKLM:\System\CurrentControlSet\Control\CrashControl -Name FilterPages -value 1
```

Health Service

The Health Service improves the day-to-day monitoring, operations, and maintenance experience of S2D clusters. This is probably one of the most important features of Windows Server 2016 to learn in relation to S2D. This is going to be your primary source of troubleshooting and diagnostic information in a failing S2D Cluster. The logging capability can be exported via API's or directly to Microsoft's Azure Operation Management Suite "OMS" via a solution provided by MVP Stanislav Zhelyazkov.

Prerequisites

The Health Service is enabled by default with Storage Spaces Direct. No additional action is required to set it up or start it.

Metrics

The Health Service reduces the work required to get live performance and capacity information from your Storage Spaces Direct cluster. One new cmdlet provides a curated list of essential metrics, which are collected efficiently and aggregated dynamically across nodes, with built-in logic to detect cluster membership. All values are real-time and point-in-time only.

Metrics

In Windows Server 2016, the Health Service provides the following metrics:

- **IOPS** (Read, Write, Total)
- **IO Throughput** (Read, Write, Total)
- **IO Latency** (Read, Write)
- **Physical Capacity** (Total, Remaining)
- **Pool Capacity** (Total, Remaining)
- **Volume Capacity** (Total, Remaining)
- **CPU Utilization** %, All Machines Average
- **Memory, All Machines** (Total, Available)

Examples

Use the following PowerShell cmdlet to get metrics for the entire Storage Spaces Direct cluster:

```
Get-StorageSubSystem Cluster* | Get-StorageHealthReport
```

The optional **Count** parameter indicates how many sets of values to return, at one second intervals.

```
Get-StorageSubSystem Cluster* | Get-StorageHealthReport -Count <Count>
```

You can also get metrics for one specific volume or node using the following cmdlets:

```
Get-Volume -FileSystemLabel <Label> | Get-StorageHealthReport -Count <Count>
Get-StorageNode -Name <Name> | Get-StorageHealthReport -Count <Count>
```

Capacity Planning

The notion of available capacity in Storage Spaces is nuanced. To help you plan effectively, the Health Service provides six distinct metrics for capacity. Here is what each represents:

- **Physical Capacity Total:** The sum of the raw capacity of all physical storage devices managed by the cluster.
- **Physical Capacity Available:** The physical capacity which is not in any non-primordial storage pool.
- **Pool Capacity Total:** The amount of raw capacity in storage pools.
- **Pool Capacity Available:** The pool capacity which is not allocated to the footprint of volumes.
- **Volume Capacity Total:** The total usable ("inside") capacity of existing volumes.
- **Volume Capacity Available:** The amount of additional data which can be stored in existing volumes.

The following diagram illustrates the relationship between these quantities.

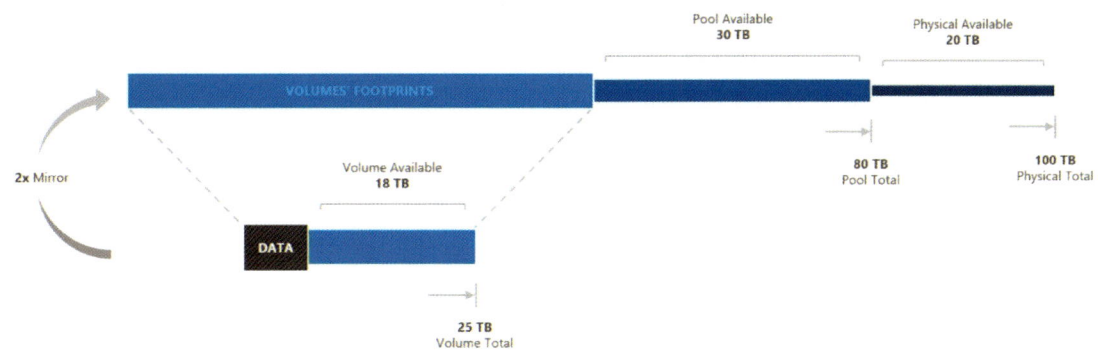

Figure 31 – Illustration of the Capacity of an S2D Cluster

Faults

The Health Service constantly monitors your Storage Spaces Direct cluster to detect problems and generate "Faults" if they find one. With a single new cmdlet Server 2016 PowerShell displays any current Faults, allowing you to easily verify the health of your deployment without looking at every entity or feature in turn. Faults are designed to be precise, easy to understand, and actionable.

Each Fault contains five important fields:

- Severity
- Description of the problem
- Recommended next step(s) to address the problem
- Identifying information for the faulting entity
- Its physical location (if applicable)

For example, here is a typical fault:

```
Severity: MINOR
Reason: Connectivity has been lost to the physical disk.
Recommendation: Check that the physical disk is working and properly
connected.
Part: Manufacturer Contoso, Model XYZ9000, Serial 123456789
Location: Seattle DC, Rack B07, Node 4, Slot 11
```

Chapter 3   Windows Server 2016 Failover Clustering

Fault Coverage

In Windows Server 2016, the Health Service provides the following Fault coverage:

Essential cluster hardware:

- Node down, quarantined, or isolated
- Node network adapter failure, disabled, or disconnected
- Node missing one or more cluster networks
- Node temperature sensor

Essential storage hardware:

- Physical disk media failure, lost connectivity, or unresponsive
- Storage enclosure lost connectivity
- Storage enclosure fan failure or power supply failure
- Storage enclosure current, voltage, or temperature sensors triggered

The Storage Spaces software stack:

- Storage pool unrecognized metadata
- Data not fully resilient, or detached
- Volume low capacity[1]

Storage Quality of Service (Storage QoS)

- Storage QoS malformed policy
- Storage QoS policy breach[2]

Chapter 3 Windows Server 2016 Failover Clustering

Storage Replica

- Replication failed to sync, write, start, or stop
- Target or source replication group failure or lost communication
- Unable to meet configured recovery point objective
- Log or metadata corruption

Health Service

- Any issues with automation, described in later sections
- Quarantined physical disk device

1 Indicates the volume has reached 80% full (minor severity) or 90% full (major severity).

2 Indicates some .vhd(s) on the volume have not met their Minimum IOPS for over 10% (minor), 30% (major), or 50% (critical) of rolling 24-hour window.

> **Note:** The health of storage enclosure components such as fans, power supplies, and sensors is derived from SCSI Enclosure Services (SES). If your vendor does not provide this information, the Health Service cannot display it.

Using the Health Service

To see any current Faults, run the following cmdlet in PowerShell:

```
Get-StorageSubSystem Cluster* | Debug-StorageSubSystem
```

You can also view Faults that are affecting only specific volumes or file shares with the following cmdlets:

```
Get-Volume -FileSystemLabel <Label> | Debug-Volume
Get-FileShare -Name <Name> | Debug-FileShare
```

This returns any Faults that affect only the specific volume or file share. Most often, these Faults relate to data resiliency or features like Storage QoS or Storage Replica.

> **Note:** In Windows Server 2016, it may take up to 30 minutes for certain Faults to appear. Improvements are forthcoming in subsequent releases.

Root Cause Analysis

The Health Service can assess the potential causality among Faulting entities to identify and combine Faults which are consequences of the same underlying problem. By recognizing chains of effect, this makes for less chatty reporting. For now, this functionality is limited to nodes, enclosures, and physical disks in the event of lost connectivity.

For example, if an enclosure has lost connectivity, it follows that those physical disk devices within the enclosure will also be without connectivity. Therefore, only one Fault will be raised for the root cause - in this case, the enclosure.

Get-StorageHealthAction

The upcoming section describes workflows which are automated by the Health Service. To verify that an action is indeed being taken autonomously, or to track its progress or outcome, the Health Service generates "Actions". Unlike logs, Actions disappear shortly after they have completed, and are intended primarily to provide insight into ongoing activity which may impact performance or capacity (e.g. restoring resiliency or rebalancing data).

One new PowerShell cmdlet displays all Actions:

```
Get-StorageHealthAction
```

In Windows Server 2016, the **Get-StorageHealthAction** cmdlet can return any of the following information:

- Retiring failed, lost connectivity, or unresponsive physical disk
- Switching storage pool to use replacement physical disk
- Restoring full resiliency to data
- Rebalancing storage pool

Disk Lifecycle

The Health Service automates most stages of the physical disk lifecycle. Let's say that the initial state of your deployment is in perfect health - which is to say, all physical disks are working properly.

Retirement

Physical disks are automatically retired when they can no longer be used, and a corresponding Fault is raised. There are several cases:

- Media Failure: the physical disk is definitively failed or broken, and must be replaced.
- Lost Communication: the physical disk has lost connectivity for over 15 consecutive minutes.
- Unresponsive: the physical disk has exhibited latency of over 5.0 seconds three or more times within an hour.

> **Note:** If connectivity is lost to many physical disks at once, or to an entire node or storage enclosure, the Health Service will not retire these disks since they are unlikely to be the root problem.

If the retired disk was serving as the cache for many other physical disks, these will automatically be reassigned to another cache disk if one is available. No special user action is required.

Restoring resiliency

Chapter 3 Windows Server 2016 Failover Clustering

Once a physical disk has been retired, the Health Service immediately begins copying its data onto the remaining physical disks, to restore full resiliency. Once this has completed, the data is completely safe and fault tolerant anew.

> **Note:** This immediate restoration requires sufficient available capacity among the remaining physical disks.

Blinking the indicator light

If possible, the Health Service will begin blinking the indicator light on the retired physical disk or its slot. This will continue indefinitely, until the retired disk is replaced.

> **Note:** In some cases, the disk may have failed in a way that precludes even its indicator light from functioning - for example, a total loss of power.

Physical replacement

You should replace the retired physical disk when possible. Most often, this consists of a hot-swap - i.e. powering off the node or storage enclosure is not required. See the Fault for helpful location and part information.

Verification

When the replacement disk is inserted, it will be verified against the Supported Components Document

Pooling

If allowed, the replacement disk is automatically substituted into its predecessor's pool to enter use. At this point, the system is returned to its initial state of perfect health, and then the Fault disappears.

Supported Components Document

The Supported Components Document is an enforcement mechanism used by the Health Service to restrict the components used by Storage Spaces Direct to those listed on the Document. The administrator or solution vendor provide the list of supported components. Using this Supported Components Document to prevent mistaken use of unsupported hardware by you or others may help with warranty or support contract compliance. At this point, only physical disk devices, including SSDs, HDDs, and NVMe drives are covered by this functionality. The Supported Components Document can restrict based on model, manufacturer (optional), and firmware version (optional).

The Supported Components Document uses an XML-inspired syntax. Your favorite text editor, such as Visual Studio Code (available for free here) or Notepad, can be used to create an XML document which you can save and reuse.

The XML document has two independent sections: **Disks** and **Cache**.

If the Disks section is provided, any unlisted drives are prevented from joining pools, which effectively precludes their use in production. If this section is left empty, any drive will be allowed to join pools.

Similarly, the Cache section governs which disks can be used for caching. If this section is left empty, Storage Spaces Direct will attempt to guess based on media type and bus type. For example, if your deployment uses solid-state drives (SSD) and hard disk drives (HDD), the former is automatically chosen for caching; however, if your deployment uses all-flash, you may need to specify the higher endurance devices you'd like to use for caching here.

```xml
<Components>
  <Disks>
    <Disk>
      <Manufacturer>Contoso</Manufacturer>
      <Model>XYZ9000</Model>
      <AllowedFirmware>
         <Version>2.0</Version>
         <Version>2.1</Version>
         <Version>2.2</Version>
      </AllowedFirmware>
      <TargetFirmware>
         <Version>2.1</Version>
         <BinaryPath>\\path\to\image.bin</BinaryPath>
      </TargetFirmware>
    </Disk>
  </Disks>
```

```xml
  <Cache>
    <Disk>
      <Manufacturer>Fabrikam</Manufacturer>
      <Model>QRSTUV</Model>
    </Disk>
  </Cache>

</Components>
```

To list multiple drives, simply add additional <Disk> tags within either section.

To inject this XML when deploying Storage Spaces Direct, use the -XML flag:

```
Enable-ClusterS2D -XML <MyXML>
```

To set or modify the Supported Components Document once Storage Spaces Direct has been deployed (i.e. once the Health Service is already running), use the following PowerShell cmdlet:

```
$MyXML = Get-Content <\\path\to\file.xml> | Out-String
Get-StorageSubSystem Cluster* | Set-StorageHealthSetting -Name
"System.Storage.SupportedComponents.Document" -Value $MyXML
```

Health Service Settings

The Health Service exposes many of the parameters governing its behavior as settings. These can be modified, whether to turn certain behaviors off/on, to tune the aggressiveness of Faults and Actions, and more.

Use the following PowerShell cmdlet to set or modify settings.

```
Get-StorageSubSystem Cluster* | Set-StorageHealthSetting -Name <SettingName> -Value <Value>
```

For example:

```
Get-StorageSubSystem Cluster* | Set-StorageHealthSetting -Name "System.Storage.Volume.CapacityThreshold.Warning" -Value 70
```

Volume Capacity Threshold

```
"System.Storage.Volume.CapacityThreshold.Enabled"  = True
"System.Storage.Volume.CapacityThreshold.Warning"  = 80
"System.Storage.Volume.CapacityThreshold.Critical" = 90
```

Pool Reserve Capacity Threshold

```
"System.Storage.StoragePool.CheckPoolReserveCapacity.Enabled" = True
```

Physical Disk Lifecycle

```
"System.Storage.PhysicalDisk.AutoPool.Enabled"                            = True
"System.Storage.PhysicalDisk.AutoRetire.OnLostCommunication.Enabled"      = True
"System.Storage.PhysicalDisk.AutoRetire.OnUnresponsive.Enabled"           = True
"System.Storage.PhysicalDisk.AutoRetire.DelayMs"                          = 900000 (i.e. 15 minutes)
"System.Storage.PhysicalDisk.Unresponsive.Reset.CountResetIntervalSeconds" = 360 (i.e. 60 minutes)
"System.Storage.PhysicalDisk.Unresponsive.Reset.CountAllowed"             = 3
```

Firmware Rollout

```
"System.Storage.PhysicalDisk.AutoFirmwareUpdate.SingleDrive.Enabled"   = True
"System.Storage.PhysicalDisk.AutoFirmwareUpdate.RollOut.Enabled"       = True
"System.Storage.PhysicalDisk.AutoFirmwareUpdate.RollOut.LongDelaySeconds"  = 604800 (i.e. 7 days)
"System.Storage.PhysicalDisk.AutoFirmwareUpdate.RollOut.ShortDelaySeconds" = 86400 (i.e. 1 day)
"System.Storage.PhysicalDisk.AutoFirmwareUpdate.RollOut.LongDelayCount"    = 1
"System.Storage.PhysicalDisk.AutoFirmwareUpdate.RollOut.FailureTolerance"  = 3
```

Platform / Quiescence

```
"Platform.Quiescence.MinDelaySeconds" = 120 (i.e. 2 minutes)
"Platform.Quiescence.MaxDelaySeconds" = 420 (i.e. 7 minutes)
```

Metrics

```
"System.Reports.ReportingPeriodSeconds" = 1
```

Debugging

```
"System.LogLevel" = 4
```

Chapter 4
S2D Networking Primer

A fundamental part of any cloud capable deployment is networking, and the Software Defined Datacenter is no different. Windows Server 2016 provides new and improved Software Defined Networking (SDN) technologies to help you move to a fully realized SDDC solution for your organization.

When you manage networks as a software defined resource, you can describe an application's infrastructure requirements one time, and then choose where the application runs - on premises or in the cloud. These consistently applied requirements and specifications mean that your applications are now easier to scale and can be seamlessly run, anywhere, with equal confidence around security, performance, quality of service, and availability.

For S2D, only a subset of these new features are required for the proper configuration and management. This chapter will focus only on the required network components to configure S2D properly. Most of the configuration issues with S2D come from incorrectly configuring the network stack. Take the time to read this section thoroughly prior to commencing your first deployment.

A big thank you to James McIllece from Microsoft for writing the Windows Server 2016 NIC and Switch Embedded Teaming User Guide that we used as a reference. The guide can be downloaded here: https://gallery.technet.microsoft.com/windows-server-2016-839cb607?redir=0

Windows Server 2016 Network Architecture

Microsoft's latest Windows Server release provides an alternative NIC Teaming solution for environments where Hyper-V is installed and the Software Defined Networking stack (SDN-stack) is being used. This solution integrates the teaming logic into the Hyper-V switch. This technology will be referred to as Switch-Embedded Teaming (SET) for the rest of this chapter.

Teaming Configurations

There are two basic configurations for NIC Teaming.

Switch-independent teaming.

With Switch-independent teaming, teaming is configured without the knowledge or participation of the switch. The switch is not aware that the network adapter is part of a team in the host, allowing the adapters the flexibility to be connected to different switches. Switch independent modes of operation do not require that the team members connect to different switches; they merely make it possible.

- **Active/Stand-by Teaming:** Rather than take advantage of the bandwidth aggregation capabilities of NIC Teaming, some administrators prefer to build in an extra layer of redundancy. These administrators choose to use one or more team members for traffic (active) and one team member to be held in reserve (stand-by) to come into action if an active team member fails. This mode of Teaming can be set by first setting the team to Switch-independent teaming, then selecting a stand-by team member through the management tool you are using. Fault-tolerance is present whether Active/Stand-by is set or not, provided there are at least two network adapters in a team. Furthermore, if your Switch Independent team has at least two members, one adapter can be marked by Windows NIC Teaming as a stand-by adapter. This stand-by adapter will only be used for inbound traffic, unless the active adapter fails. Inbound traffic (e.g., broadcast packets) received on the stand-by adapter will be delivered up the stack. Once the failed team member or team members are restored, the stand-by team member will return to stand-by status.

    Once a stand-by member of a team is connected to the network all network resources required to service traffic on the member are in place and active. While Active/Standby configuration provides administrators with peace of mind, clients will see better network utilization and lower latency by operating their teams with all team members active. In a Failover situation, the redistribution of traffic across the remaining healthy team members will occur anytime one or more of the team members reports an error state, whether adapters are set to active or not.

Switch-dependent teaming.

As you might have guessed, this second option requires the participation of the switch. All members of the team must be connected to the same physical switch. There are two modes of operation for switch-dependent teaming:

- **Generic or static teaming (IEEE 802.3ad draft v1):** Both the switch and the host require configuration for this mode to function. It is a statically configured solution, and for that reason, there is no additional protocol to assist the switch and the host to identify incorrectly plugged cables or other errors that could cause the team to fail to perform. Typically, this mode is supported by and used for server-class switches.

- **Link Aggregation Control Protocol teaming (IEEE 802.1ax, LACP).** This mode is also commonly referred to as IEEE 802.3ad as it was developed in the IEEE 802.3ad committee before being published as IEEE 802.1ax. This mode uses the Link Aggregation Control Protocol (LACP) to dynamically identify links that are connected between the host and a given switch. Teams are thus automatically created, and in theory (but rarely in practice), the team can be expanded or reduced simply by the transmission or receipt of LACP packets from the peer entity. IEEE 802.1ax is supported by typical server-class switches, but most require the network operator to administratively enable LACP on the port. Windows NIC Teaming always operates in LACP's Active mode with a short timer. No option is presently available to modify the timer or change the LACP mode.

The above modes both allow both inbound and outbound traffic to approach the practical limits of the aggregated bandwidth because the pool of team members is seen as a single pipe.

Inbound load distribution is governed by the switch. For this reason, it is important to research the options available for inbound load distribution management. For example, a good number of switches only support destination IP address to team member mapping, resulting in a less granular distribution than is needed for a good inbound load distribution. Covering all the settings on all switches is not feasible in this guide, so it remains up to the reader to research and understand the capabilities of the adjacent network switches in their environment.

In Windows Server 2016

- Stand-alone NIC Teaming supports all these modes;
- Switch-embedded NIC Teaming supports Switch Independent mode with no stand-by team members.

> **Note:** If you have previously configured your environments using Switch-Dependent Teaming (LACP) configurations. These are no longer supported for S2D deployments, and you will need to move your configurations to 100 % Switch Independent. S2D provides a required feature called Remote Direct Memory Access (RDMA). This feature is not compatible with Switch-Dependent teaming. For the balance of this chapter we will not be discussing any further configurations of Switch Dependent or LBFO teaming. SET teaming is the first teaming technology from Microsoft that supports RDMA natively inside the team. In previous versions like 2012 R2 you could not team your adapters if you wanted to use RDMA.

Algorithms for load distribution

Distribution of outbound traffic among the available links can be configured in many ways. A rule-of-thumb governing any distribution algorithm is to try to keep all packets associated with a single flow (TCP-stream) on a single network adapter. This minimizes performance degradation caused by reassembling out-of-order TCP segments.

Stand-alone NIC teaming supports the following traffic load distribution algorithms:

- **Hyper-V switch port:** Because virtual machines are each assigned independent MAC addresses, the MAC Address or the port it is connected to on the Hyper-V switch can be the basis for dividing traffic. This scheme can be advantageous in virtualization. The adjacent switch sees a particular MAC Address connected to only one port, allowing the switch to automatically distribute the ingress load (the traffic from the switch to the host) on multiple links based on the destination MAC (VM MAC) address. This is particularly useful when Virtual Machine Queues (VMQs) can be placed on the specific NIC where the traffic is expected to arrive. However, if the host has only a few VMs, this mode may not be granular enough to obtain a well-balanced distribution. This mode will also always limit a single VM (i.e., the traffic from a single switch port) to the bandwidth available on a single interface. Windows Server 2012 R2 uses the Hyper-V Switch Port as the identifier rather than the source MAC address as, in some instances, a VM may be using more than one MAC address on a switch port.
- **Address Hashing:** An algorithm is used to create a hash based on address components of the packet and then assigns packets with that particular hash value to one of the available adapters. This mechanism alone is usually sufficient to create a reasonable balance across the available adapters.

    The components that can be specified, using PowerShell, as inputs to the hashing function include the following:
    - Source and destination TCP ports and source and destination IP addresses (this is used by the user interface when "Address Hash" is selected)
    - Source and destination IP addresses only

- o Source and destination MAC addresses only

The TCP ports hash creates the most granular distribution of traffic streams, resulting in smaller streams that can be independently moved between members. However, it cannot be used for traffic that is not TCP or UDP-based, nor can it be used where the TCP and UDP ports are hidden from the stack, such as IPsec-protected traffic. In these cases, the hash automatically falls back to the IP address hash or, if the traffic is not IP traffic, to the MAC address hash.

- **Dynamic.** The best aspects of the previous two modes are combined in this algorithm:
    - o A hash is created based on TCP ports and IP addresses, and is used to distribute outbound loads. Also, in Dynamic mode, loads are rebalanced in real time so that a given outbound flow may move back and forth between team members.
    - o For inbound loads, distribution occurs as if the Hyper-V port mode was in use.

The outbound loads in this mode are dynamically balanced based on the concept of "flowlets". TCP flows have naturally occurring breaks, much like the natural breaks between words and sentences found in human speech. A flowlet is the 'body' of a particular portion of the TCP flow, or the packet-flow between two such breaks. The dynamic mode algorithm detects these flowlet boundaries (the boundary being any break in the packet flow of sufficient length), and redistributes the flow to the least-taxed team member as appropriate. If flows do not contain any discernible flowlets, the algorithm may periodically rebalance flows regardless, if circumstances require it. The dynamic balancing algorithm can change the affinity between TCP flow and team member at any time as it works to balance the workload of the team members.

Switch-embedded Teaming supports only the Hyper-V switch port and Dynamic load distribution algorithms.

Note: From our experience Dynamic is the preferred choice 99% of the time. It is even recommended by Microsoft Consulting Services (MCS) in most cases.

Converged Network Interface Card (NIC)

With the Converged Network Interface Card (NIC), a single network adapter can be used for management, Remote Direct Memory Access (RDMA)-enabled storage, and tenant traffic. This allows you to use fewer network adapters to manage different types of traffic, potentially reducing overall capital expenditure.

Switch Independent / Address Hash

With this configuration, loads are distributed through the selected level of address hashing. TCP ports and IP addresses are used by default to seed the hash function.

Because a given IP address can only be associated with a single MAC address for routing purposes, this mode essentially restricts inbound traffic to only one team member (the primary member). This means that the inbound traffic is limited to the bandwidth of one team member no matter how much is getting sent.

This mode is best used for teaming in a VM.

Switch Independent / Hyper-V Port

In this configuration, packets are sent using all active team members, distributing the load based on the Hyper-V switch port number. Bandwidth will be limited to not more than one team member's bandwidth because the port is affinitized to exactly one team member at any point in time.

With the Hyper-V port associated to only a single team member, inbound traffic for the VM's switch port is received on the same team member the switch port's outbound traffic uses. This also allows maximum use of Virtual Machine Queues (VMQs) for better performance over all.

Hyper-V Port configuration is best used only when teaming NICs that operate at or above 10Gbps. For high bit-rate NICS such as these, Hyper-V port distribution mode may provide better performance than Dynamic distribution. In all other cases where Hyper-V port was recommended in previous Windows Server versions, Switch-Independent/Dynamic, covered next, will provide better performance.

Switch Independent / Dynamic

With Switch-Independent/Dynamic mode, the load is distributed based on a TCP ports hash modified by the Dynamic load-balancing algorithm. The algorithm redistributes flows to optimize team member bandwidth utilization, and, as a result, individual flow transmissions may move from one active team member to another. When redistributing traffic, there is always a small possibility that out-of-order delivery could occur, but the dynamic algorithm takes that into account and takes steps to minimize that possibility.

On the receiving side, distribution will look identical to Hyper-V port mode. The traffic of each Hyper-V switch port, whether bound for a virtual NIC in a VM (vmNIC) or a virtual NIC in the host (vNIC), will see all inbound traffic arriving on a single NIC.

This mode is best used for teaming in both native and Hyper-V environments except when:

Chapter 4   S2D Networking Primer

- Teaming is being performed in a VM,
- Switch dependent teaming (e.g., LACP) is required by policy, or
- Operation of an Active/Stand-by team is required by policy.

Switch Embedded Teaming (SET)

Switch Embedded Teaming is a NIC Teaming solution that is integrated in the Hyper-V Virtual Switch. Up to eight physical NICS can be added into a single SET team, improving availability and ensuring failover. Windows Server 2016 lets you create SET teams that are restricted to the use of Server Message Block (SMB) and RDMA. In addition, SET teams can be used to distribute network traffic for Hyper-V Network Virtualization.

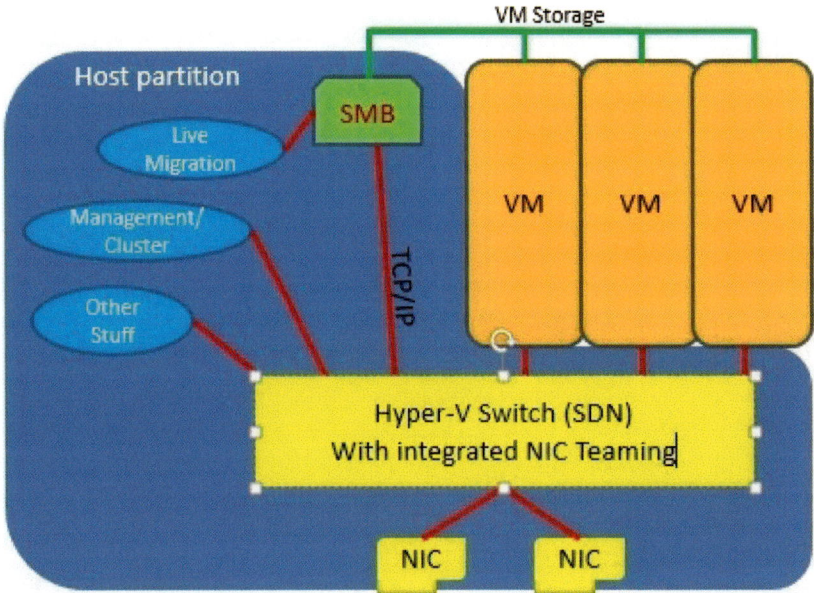

Figure 32 – SET Architecture

SET cannot be used in a virtual machine, as it is integrated into the Hyper-V Virtual Switch. However, you can use other forms of NIC Teaming within said VMs.

Another benefit to SET architecture is that it does not expose team interfaces. Instead, you must configure Hyper-V Virtual Switch ports.

SET Availability

If your version of Windows Server 2016 includes Hyper-V and the SDN stack, SET is available. Windows PowerShell commands and Remote Desktop connections are available to let you manage SET from remote computers that are running a client operating system upon which the tools are supported.

SET Supported NICs

Any Ethernet NIC that is trusted and certified by the Windows Hardware Qualification and Logo (WHQL) test can be added in a SET team in Windows Server 2016. All network adapters that are members of a SET team must be of an identical make and model (same manufacturer, model, firmware and driver). As stated earlier, SET supports anywhere from one up to eight network adapters in a team.

SET Compatibility

SET is compatible with the following networking technologies in Windows Server 2016.

- Datacenter bridging (DCB)

- Hyper-V Network Virtualization - NV-GRE and VxLAN are both supported in Windows Server 2016.

- Receive-side Checksum offloads (IPv4, IPv6, TCP) - These are supported if any of the SET team members support them.

- Remote Direct Memory Access (RDMA)

- Single root I/O virtualization (SR-IOV)

- Transmit-side Checksum offloads (IPv4, IPv6, TCP) - These are supported if all of the SET team members support them.

- Virtual Machine Queues (VMQ)

- Virtual Receive Side Scaling (RSS)

SET is not compatible with the following networking technologies in Windows Server 2016.

- 802.1X authentication

- IPsec Task Offload (IPsecTO)

- QoS in host or native operating systems

- Receive side coalescing (RSC)
- Receive side scaling (RSS)
- TCP Chimney Offload
- Virtual Machine QoS (VM-QoS)

SET Modes and Settings

When creating a SET Team, unlike NIC Teaming, a team name cannot be configured. Another difference between SET and standard NIC Teaming is that stand-by adapters cannot be used in SET. When you deploy SET, all network adapters must be active. Also, NIC Teaming provides three different teaming modes, while SET only supports **Switch Independent**.

With **Switch Independent** mode, the switch or switches to which the SET Team members are connected are unaware of the presence of the SET team and do not determine how to distribute network traffic to SET team members - instead, the SET team distributes inbound network traffic across the SET team members.

When you create a new SET team, you must configure the following team properties.

- Member adapters
- Load balancing mode

Member Adapters

When you create a SET team, you must specify up to eight identical network adapters that are bound to the Hyper-V Virtual Switch as SET team member adapters.

Load Balancing Modes for SET

The options for SET team Load Balancing distribution mode are **Hyper-V** Port and **Dynamic.**

Note: When you use SET in conjunction with Packet Direct, the teaming mode Switch Independent and the load balancing mode Hyper-V Port are required.

SET and Virtual Machine Queues (VMQs)

VMQ and SET work well together, and you should enable VMQ whenever you are using Hyper-V and SET.

> **Note:** SET always presents the total number of queues that are available across all SET team members. In NIC Teaming, this is called Sum-of-Queues mode.

Most network adapters have queues that can be used for either Receive Side Scaling (RSS) or VMQ, but not both at the same time.

Some VMQ settings appear to be settings for RSS queues but are really settings on the generic queues that both RSS and VMQ use depending on which feature is presently in use. Each NIC has, in its advanced properties, values for *RssBaseProcNumber and *MaxRssProcessors.

Following are a few VMQ settings that provide better system performance:

- Ideally each NIC should have the *RssBaseProcNumber set to an even number greater than or equal to two (2). This is because the first physical processor, Core 0 (logical processors 0 and 1), typically does most of the system processing so the network processing should be steered away from this physical processor.

> **Note:** Some machine architectures don't have two logical processors per physical processor, so for such machines the base processor should be greater than or equal to 1. If in doubt, assume your host is using a 2 logical processor per physical processor architecture.

- The team members' processors should be, to the extent that it's practical, non-overlapping. For example, in a 4-core host (8 logical processors) with a team of 2 10Gbps NICs, you could set the first one to use base processor of 2 and to use 4 cores; the second would be set to use base processor 6 and use 2 cores.

SET and Hyper-V Network Virtualization

SET is fully compatible with Hyper-V Network Virtualization in Windows Server 2016. The HNV management system provides information to the SET driver that allows SET to distribute the network traffic load in a manner that is optimized for the HNV traffic.

SET and Live Migration

The use of SET teams and Live Migration is fully supported in Windows Server 2016.

MAC Address Use on Transmitted Packets

When a SET team is configured with dynamic load distribution, the packets from a single source (such as a single VM) are simultaneously distributed across multiple team members.

SET replaces the source MAC address with a different MAC Address on the frames transmitted on team members other than the affinitized team member. This prevents the switches from getting confused and prevents MAC flapping alarms. For this reason, each team member uses a different MAC address, preventing MAC address conflicts unless and until failure occurs.

If a failure occurs on the primary NIC, and is detected by SET, the teaming software uses the VM's MAC address on the team member that is chosen to serve as the temporary affinitized team member (i.e., the one that will now appear to the switch as the VM's interface).

This MAC Address change only applies to traffic that was going to be sent on the VM's affinitized team member with the VM's own MAC address as its source MAC address. Other traffic continues to be sent with whatever source MAC address it would have used prior to the failure.

Following are lists that describe SET teaming MAC address replacement behavior, based on how the team is configured:

In Switch Independent mode with Hyper-V Port distribution

- Every vmSwitch port is affinitized to a team member

- Every packet is sent on the team member to which the port is affinitized

- No source MAC replacement is done

In Switch Independent mode with Dynamic distribution

- Every vmSwitch port is affinitized to a team member

- All ARP/NS packets are sent on the team member to which the port is affinitized

- Packets sent on the team member that is the affinitized team member have no source MAC address replacement done

- Packets sent on a team member other than the affinitized team member will have source MAC address replacement done

SET vs. LBFO Teaming

The table below is a comparison of the features supported by LBFO Teaming and SET Teaming.

LBFO/SET Feature comparison

Feature	LBFO	SET	Feature interactions: works with	LBFO	SET
Switch independent teaming	✓	✓	Checksum offloads	✓	✓
Switch dependent teaming: Static	✓	✗	DCB	⚠	✓
Switch dependent teaming: LACP	✓	✗	HNV v1	✓	✗
Dynamic load distribution	✓	✓	HNV v2	✗	✗
HyperVPort mode load distribution	✓	✓	IEEE 802.1X	✓	✓
Address hash load distribution	✓	✗	IPsecTO	✗	✗
Active/Standby operation	✓	✗	LSO	✓	✓
Teams of up to ___ members	32	8	RDMA	✗	✓
VMM managed	✓	RTM	RSC	✗	✗
Inbox UI managed	✓	✗	RSS	✗	✓
PowerShell managed	✓	✓	SDN-QoS	✗	✓
Works in Native stack	✓	✗	SR-IOV	✗	✓
Works in a VM	✓	✓	TCP Chimney	✗	✗
Teams different speed NICs	✓	✗	VMMQ	✗	✓
Teams different NICs	✓	✗	VMQ (filter)	✓	✗
vNICs/vmNICs affinitized to team members	✗	✓	VMQ (NIC Switch)	✗	✓
			vmQoS	✗	✗
			vRSS	✓	✓

Figure 33 – LBFO vs. SET Feature Comparison

Managing SET Teams

Switch-embedded teams are best managed using the Virtual Machine Manager (VMM).

In the event an administrator prefers to use PowerShell to manage a switch-embedded team, here are the cmdlets to use.

Creating a SET Team

A switch-embedded team must be created at the time the Hyper-V switch is created. When creating the Hyper-V switch using the **New-VMSwitch** PowerShell cmdlet, the "EnableEmbeddedTeaming" option must be selected.

For example, the PowerShell cmdlet shown here:

```
New-VMSwitch -Name TeamedvSwitch -NetAdapterName "NIC 1","NIC 2" -EnableEmbeddedTeaming $true
```

will create a Hyper-V switch named TeamedvSwitch with embedded teaming and two initial team members.

Adding or removing a member of a SET team

The **Set-VMSwitchTeam** cmdlet has a **-NetAdapterName <string[]>** option. To change the team members in a switch embedded team enter the desired list of team members after the **NetAdapterName** option. If using the team created in the previous example, the cmdlet

```
Set-VMSwitch -Name TeamedvSwitch -NetAdapterName "NIC 1","NIC 3"
```

will delete team member "NIC 2" and add a new team member labelled "NIC 3".

Alternatively, the **Add-VMSwitchTeamMember** and **Remove-VMSwitchTeamMember** cmdlets may be used.

Removing a SET team

A switch-embedded team can only be removed by removing the Hyper-V switch that contains it. Use the **Remove-VMSwitch** cmdlet to remove the Hyper-V switch.

Changing the load distribution algorithm of a SET team

The **Set-VMSwitchTeam** cmdlet has a **-LoadBalancingAlgorithm <VMSwitchLoadBalancingAlgorithm>** option. This option takes one of two possible values: **HyperVPort**, or **Dynamic**. To set or change the load distribution algorithm for a switch-embedded team use this option. For example,

```
Set-VMSwitch -Name TeamedvSwitch -VMSwitchLoadBalancingAlgorithm Dynamic
```

Forcing the affinity of a VM or vNIC to a physical NIC

Windows Server 2016 allows the host administrator to force a host vNIC or a vmNIC to be affinitized to a particular team member. While there are few good reasons to do this, a number of customers have requested this feature in order, for example, to try to ensure that traffic from a given vNIC, e.g., a storage vNIC, uses a particular NIC to send traffic so that it passes through a shorter path to the storage server.

Setting an affinity will not prevent failover to another physical NIC if the selected NIC encounters failures. The affinity will be restored when the selected NIC is restored to operation.

Setting up an affinity between a vNIC and a Physical NIC

The PowerShell cmdlet Set-VMNetworkAdapterTeamMapping will establish an affinity between a virtual NIC (vNIC or vmNIC) and a team member. For example:

```
Set-VMNetworkAdapterTeamMapping -VMNetworkAdapterName SMB1 -ManagementOS -PhysicalNetAdapterName Ethernet2
```

will force the traffic from vNIC SMB1 to be sent and received on physical adapter Ethernet2. Similarly,

```
Set-VMNetworkAdapterTeamMapping -VMName Foo -PhysicalNetAdapterName Ethernet2
```

will force the traffic from the VM named Foo to be sent and received on physical adapter Ethernet2.

Run **Get-Help Set-VMNetworkAdapterTeamMapping** for complete details.

Checking the affinity between a vNIC and a Physical NIC

The ability to establish an affinity would be remiss if there was no way to check and see what affinities have been established. Checking the current affinities can be accomplished using the **Get-VMNetworkAdapterTeamMapping** PowerShell cmdlet.

Run **Get-Help Get-VMNetworkAdapterTeamMapping** for complete details.

Removing the affinity between a vNIC and a Physical NIC

If an affinity is no longer desired it can be removed using the **Remove-VMNetworkAdapterTeamMapping** PowerShell cmdlet.

Run **Get-Help Remove-VMNetworkAdapterTeamMapping** for complete details.

Configuring RDMA for S2D

In Windows Server 2012 R2 it is not possible to bind RMDA Services to a Hyper-V Virtual Switch or Virtual Adapter. This increases the number of physical network adapters that are required to be installed in the Hyper-V host.

In Windows Server 2016, you can use fewer network adapters while using RDMA with or without SET.

The image below illustrates the software architecture changes between Windows Server 2012 R2 and Windows Server 2016.

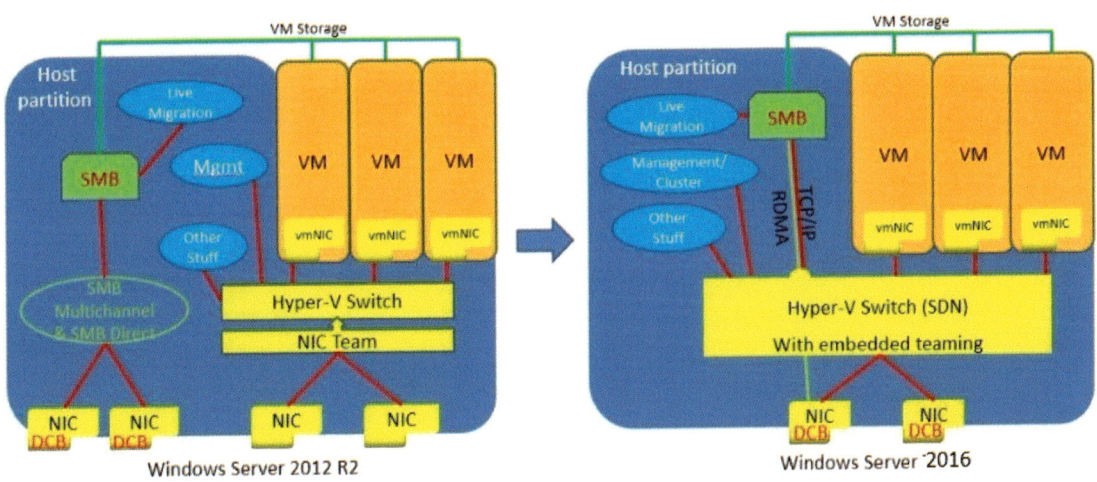

Figure 34 – RDMA Architecture in Windows Server 2016

The following sections provide instructions on how to use Windows PowerShell commands to enable Datacenter Bridging (DCB), create a Hyper-V Virtual Switch with an RDMA virtual NIC (vNIC), and create a Hyper-V Virtual Switch with SET and RDMA vNICs.

Enable Datacenter Bridging (DCB)

Before using any RDMA over Converged Ethernet (RoCE) version of RDMA, you must enable DCB. While not required for Internet Wide Area RDMA Protocol (iWARP) networks, testing has determined that all Ethernet-based RDMA technologies work better with DCB. Because of this, you should consider using DCB even for iWARP RDMA deployments.

The following Windows PowerShell script provides an example of how to enable and configure DCB for SMB Direct:

```powershell
#
# Turn on DCB
Install-WindowsFeature Data-Center-Bridging
#
# Set a policy for SMB-Direct
New-NetQosPolicy "SMB" -NetDirectPortMatchCondition 445 -PriorityValue8021Action 3
#
# Turn on Flow Control for SMB
Enable-NetQosFlowControl    -Priority 3
#
# Make sure flow control is off for other traffic
Disable-NetQosFlowControl    -Priority 0,1,2,4,5,6,7
#
# Apply policy to the target adapters
Enable-NetAdapterQos    -Name "SLOT 2"
#
# Give SMB Direct 30% of the bandwidth minimum
New-NetQosTrafficClass "SMB"    -Priority 3    -BandwidthPercentage 30    -Algorithm ETS
```

If you have a kernel debugger installed in the system, you must configure the debugger to allow QoS to be set by running the following command.

```powershell
# Override the Debugger - by default the debugger blocks NetQos
#
Set-ItemProperty HKLM:"\SYSTEM\CurrentControlSet\Services\NDIS\Parameters" AllowFlowControlUnderDebugger -type DWORD -Value 1 -Force
```

Create a Hyper-V Virtual Switch with SET and RDMA vNICs

To make use of RDMA capabilies on Hyper-V host virtual network adapters (vNICs) on a Hyper-V Virtual Switch that supports RDMA teaming, you can use the below sample Windows PowerShell script.

```powershell
#
# Create a vmSwitch with SET
#
New-VMSwitch -Name SETswitch -NetAdapterName "SLOT 2","SLOT 3" -EnableEmbeddedTeaming $true
#
# Add host vNICs and make them RDMA capable
#
Add-VMNetworkAdapter -SwitchName SETswitch -Name SMB_1 -managementOS
Add-VMNetworkAdapter -SwitchName SETswitch -Name SMB_2 -managementOS
Enable-NetAdapterRDMA "vEthernet (SMB_1)","vEthernet (SMB_2)"
#
# Verify RDMA capabilities; ensure that the capabilities are non-zero
#
Get-NetAdapterRdma | fl *
#
# Many switches won't pass traffic class information on untagged VLAN traffic,
# so make sure host adapters for RDMA are on VLANs. (This example assigns the two SMB_*
# host virtual adapters to VLAN 42.)
#
Set-VMNetworkAdapterIsolation -ManagementOS -VMNetworkAdapterName SMB_1 -IsolationMode VLAN -DefaultIsolationID 42
Set-VMNetworkAdapterIsolation -ManagementOS -VMNetworkAdapterName SMB_2 -IsolationMode VLAN -DefaultIsolationID 42
```

Chapter 5
Deploying Storage Spaces Direct (S2D)

The day has arrived for your company to start deploying it's newly acquired HyperConveged Infrastructure from SuperMicro. Fortunately, the Out of Box experience process has been greatly simplified and a near instant-on infrastructure can be achieved. Your Vendor has pre-imaged all of the nodes with a copy of Windows Server 2016 Datacenter edition. As you follow through this chapter we will walk you through the post-configuration steps necessary to deploy a hyper-converged Storage Spaces Direct configuration.

One box arrived today at your company's headquarters in Calgary, AB, Canada. Currently all that is configured in the rack at the datacenter is the following:

- 2 x 15 Amp APC PDU (Power Distribution Units)
- 2 x Top of Rack Cisco Nexus 9372x Switches
- 2 x APC Rack Mount UPS

The next step was unboxing the Supermicro Superserver 2028TP-HC0TR. This is a very common model used by other hyper-converged vendors such as Nutanix. The nice thing about this unit is that it is readily available and the post configuration steps are quite straight forward.

Figure 35 – Supermicro Superserver 2028TP-HC0TR front view

Chapter 5   Deploying Storage Spaces Direct (S2D)

Figure 36 – Supermicro Superserver 2028TP-HC0TR rear view

Chapter 5 Deploying Storage Spaces Direct (S2D)

Figure 37 – System view of Supermicro Superserver

Chapter 5 Deploying Storage Spaces Direct (S2D)

Figure 38 – Individual node view

Chapter 5 Deploying Storage Spaces Direct (S2D)

For the purpose of this book we used an online configurator from a Supermicro reseller in the United States. This can be used as a sample configuration. This one had a few extra components in it like a APC UPS and the Windows 2016 licensing.

	SuperServer 2028TP-HC0R Configured Price: $48,161.00
Selection Summary	
Barebone	Supermicro SuperServer 2028TP-HC0TR - 2U TwinPro2 - 24x SATA/SAS - Dual 10-Gigabit Ethernet - LSI 3008 12G SAS - 2000W Redundant
Processor	8 x Eight-Core Intel Xeon Processor E5-2620 v4 2.10GHz 20MB Cache (85W)
Memory	32 x 32GB PC4-19200 2400MHz DDR4 ECC Registered DIMM
Boot Drive	128GB SATA 6.0Gb/s Disk on Module (MLC) (Vertical)
Hard Drive	16 x 900GB SAS 3.0 12.0Gb/s 10000RPM - 2.5" - Hitachi Ultrastar C10K1800 (512n) 8 x 960GB Samsung PM863a Series 2.5 SATA 6.0Gb/s Solid State Drive
Optical Drive	No Optical Drive Support
Network Card	4 x Mellanox 10-Gigabit Ethernet Adapter ConnectX-3 EN MCX312A (2x SFP+)
Power Protection	APC Smart-UPS 5000VA LCD 208V - 5U Rackmount
Operating System	4 x Microsoft Windows Server 2016 Datacenter (16-core)
Warranty	3 Year Advanced Parts Replacement Warranty and NBD Onsite Service
Tech Specs	
Barebone	
Memory Technology	DDR4 ECC Reg
North Bridge	Intel C612
Form Factor	2U
Color	Black
Memory Slots	16x 288-pin DIMM Sockets (per node)
Graphics	ASPEED AST2400 BMC
Ethernet	Intel X540 Dual port 10GBase-T (per node)

Power	2000W Redundant Platinum High-efficiency Power Supply
External Bays	6x 2.5" Hot-swap SATA/SAS Drive Bays (per node)
Expansion Slots	1x PCI Express 3.0 x16 low-profile slot (per node)
Front Panel	Power On/Off button System Reset button UID button Power status LED HDD activity LED 2x Network activity LEDs Universal Information (UID) LED
Back Panel	2x USB 3.0 ports 2x RJ45 10GBase-T ports 1x RJ45 Dedicated IPMI LAN port 1x VGA port 1x Fast UART 16550 port
Dimensions (WxHxD)	17.25" (438mm) x 3.47" (88mm) x 28.5" (724mm)
SAS 12Gbps Controller	LSI 3008
SAS 12Gbps Ports	24 (6 per node)
SATA 6Gbps AHCI Controller	Intel C612
SATA 6Gbps AHCI Ports	24 (6 per node)
SATA 6Gbps SCU Controller	sSATA
SATA 6Gbps SCU Ports	16 (4 per node)
Processor	
Product Line	Xeon E5-2600 v4
Socket	LGA2011-v3 Socket
Clock Speed	2.10 GHz
QuickPath Interconnect	8.0 GT/s
Smart Cache	20MB
Cores/Threads	8C / 16T
Intel Virtualization	Yes

Chapter 5 Deploying Storage Spaces Direct (S2D)

Technology	
Intel Hyper-Threading	Yes
Wattage	85W
Memory	
Technology	DDR4
Type	288-pin DIMM
Capacity	32 x 32 GB
Speed	2400 MHz
Error Checking	ECC
Signal Processing	Registered
Boot Drive	
Storage Capacity	128GB
Interface	6.0Gb/s Serial ATA
Hard Drive	
Storage Capacity	16 x 900GB 8 x 960GB
Interface	12.0Gb/s SAS 6.0Gb/s Serial ATA
Rotational Speed	10,000RPM
Cache	128MB
Format	512n
Endurance	1.3x DWPD
Read IOPS	97,000 IOPS (4KB)
Write IOPS	24,000 IOPS (4KB)
Read Speed	520 MB/s
Write Speed	480 MB/s
NAND	3D V-NAND
Network Card	
Transmission Speed	10-Gbps Ethernet
Port Interface	SFP+

Chapter 5   Deploying Storage Spaces Direct (S2D)

Host Interface	PCI Express 3.0 x8
Cable Medium	Copper

The SuperMicro server has been racked and wired as shown in the diagram below:

Figure 39 – Wiring Configuration Cisco Nexus 9372x

Cisco Nexus 9372x Switch Configuration

Windows 2016 uses a feature called SMB Direct, which supports the use of network adapters that have RDMA capabilities. Network adapters that support RDMA can function at full speed with very low latency, while using very little CPU. When used for workloads like Hyper-V or SQL Server this can actually resemble locally attached storage.

All of the components listed earlier in this chapter support SMB Direct and RDMA. So, let's go ahead and proceed with the switch configuration. If you remember SET teaming doesn't support LACP also known as EtherChannel. So, we will configure the Switch Ports as trunk ports only.

We will use the following VLAN's in this configuration:

VLAN	VLAN Name	VLAN Description
2	VLAN2-Backup	Backup and Replication
4	VLAN4-SMB3	SMB3 Dedicated VLAN
8	VLAN8-	Hyper-V Live Migration

		LiveMigration
9	VLAN9-CSV	Cluster Communication
10	VLAN10-MGMT	Management VLAN

```
# Create VLANs the for Switches
SWITCH#configure terminal
SWITCH(config)#vlan 2
SWITCH(config-vlan)#name VLAN2-Backup
SWITCH(config-vlan)#exit
SWITCH(config)#vlan 4
SWITCH(config-vlan)#name VLAN4-SMB3
SWITCH(config-vlan)#exit
SWITCH(config)#vlan 8
SWITCH(config)#name VLAN8-LiveMigration
SWITCH(config-vlan)#exit
SWITCH(config)#vlan 9
SWITCH(config-vlan)#name VLAN9-CSV
SWITCH(config-vlan)#exit
SWITCH(config)#vlan 10
SWITCH(config-vlan)#name VLAN10-MGMT
SWITCH(config-vlan)#exit
# Assigning IP addresses to VLANs
SWITCH#configure terminal
SWITCH(config)#interface vlan 10
SWITCH(config-if)#ip address 10.0.10.212 255.255.255.0
SWITCH(config-if)#exit
# Assigning SWITCH1 Interfaces to VLANs
switch#configure terminal
switch(config)#Interface Ethernet1/1
switch(config-if)#description S2D Node A - Riser P1
switch(config-if)#switchport trunk encapsulation dot1q
switch(config-if)# switchport trunk native vlan 10
switch(config-if)# switchport trunk allowed vlan 2 to 10
switch(config-if)# switchport mode trunk
switch(config-if)#no shut
switch(config-if)#exit
switch(config)#Interface Ethernet1/2
switch(config-if)#description S2D Node B - Riser P1
switch(config-if)#switchport trunk encapsulation dot1q
switch(config-if)# switchport trunk native vlan 10
switch(config-if)# switchport trunk allowed vlan 2 to 10
switch(config-if)# switchport mode trunk
switch(config-if)#no shut
switch(config-if)#exit
switch(config)#Interface Ethernet1/3
switch(config-if)#description S2D Node C - Riser P1
switch(config-if)#switchport trunk encapsulation dot1q
switch(config-if)# switchport trunk native vlan 10
switch(config-if)# switchport trunk allowed vlan 2 to 10
switch(config-if)# switchport mode trunk
switch(config-if)#no shut
```

Chapter 5 Deploying Storage Spaces Direct (S2D)

```
switch(config-if)#exit
switch(config)#Interface Ethernet1/4
switch(config-if)#description S2D Node D - Riser P1
switch(config-if)#switchport trunk encapsulation dot1q
switch(config-if)# switchport trunk native vlan 10
switch(config-if)# switchport trunk allowed vlan 2 to 10
switch(config-if)# switchport mode trunk
switch(config-if)#no shut
switch(config-if)#exit

# Assigning SWITCH2 Interfaces to VLANs

switch#configure terminal
switch(config)#Interface Ethernet1/1
switch(config-if)#description S2D Node A - Riser P2
switch(config-if)#switchport trunk encapsulation dot1q
switch(config-if)# switchport trunk native vlan 10
switch(config-if)# switchport trunk allowed vlan 2 to 10
switch(config-if)# switchport mode trunk
switch(config-if)#no shut
switch(config-if)#exit
switch(config)#Interface Ethernet1/2
switch(config-if)#description S2D Node B - Riser P2
switch(config-if)#switchport trunk encapsulation dot1q
switch(config-if)# switchport trunk native vlan 10
switch(config-if)# switchport trunk allowed vlan 2 to 10
switch(config-if)# switchport mode trunk
switch(config-if)#no shut
switch(config-if)#exit
switch(config)#Interface Ethernet1/3
switch(config-if)#description S2D Node C - Riser P2
switch(config-if)#switchport trunk encapsulation dot1q
switch(config-if)# switchport trunk native vlan 10
switch(config-if)# switchport trunk allowed vlan 2 to 10
switch(config-if)# switchport mode trunk
switch(config-if)#no shut
switch(config-if)#exit
switch(config)#Interface Ethernet1/4
switch(config-if)#description S2D Node D - Riser P2
switch(config-if)#switchport trunk encapsulation dot1q
switch(config-if)# switchport trunk native vlan 10
switch(config-if)# switchport trunk allowed vlan 2 to 10
switch(config-if)# switchport mode trunk
switch(config-if)#no shut
switch(config-if)#exit
```

For the final configuration, we will configure an Inter-Switch Link (ISL) between our pair of switches to support the redundant cabling configuration. These will be connected using 2 x of the 40 Gbps QSFP+ cables.

RDMA over Converged Ethernet (RoCE) requires that the fabric be configured in a lossless configuration. This is typically not possible as the TCP protocol has been designed as a best effort transport protocol. To get around this we will need to enable Datacenter Bridging (DCB) on the Windows Server 2016 hosts. Datacenter Bridging is a set of enhancements to IP Ethernet, which is designed to eliminate loss due to queue overflow, as well as to allocate bandwidth between various traffic types.

To sort out priorities and provide lossless performance for certain traffic types, DCB relies on Priority Flow Control (PFC). Rather than using the typical Global Pause method of standard Ethernet, PFC specifies individual pause parameters for eight separate priority classes. Since the priority class data is contained within the VLAN tag of any given traffic, VLAN tagging is also a requirement for RoCE and, therefore SMB Direct.

There is a great configuration guide that has been published by Lenovo that demonstrates this exact configuration on their gear at: https://lenovopress.com/lp0064.pdf.

In future volumes of the book we will show multiple configurations with multiple vendors.

Powering on the S2D nodes

When these units were shipped from the factory they were pre-imaged with Windows Server 2016 Data Center Edition. This means that for the purpose of this book all we needed to do was turn on the nodes to commence configuration.

Figure 40 – Powering on the S2D Nodes

IPMI Configuration

When we ordered the HyperConverged Appliances we asked to have the IPMI (Itelligient Platform Mangement Interface) pre-configured. The IP Addresses for the IPMI Interfaces on each of the nodes are shown in the table below:

Node	IPMI IPAddress
S2DNODE1	10.10.240.11
S2DNODE2	10.10.240.12
S2DNODE3	10.10.240.13
S2DNODE4	10.10.240.14

Note: IPMI (Intelligent Platform Management Interface) is similar to Hewlett Packard (HP) ILO (Integrated Lights-Out) or Dell's IDRAC (Integrated Dell Remote Access)

> **Note:** To access the IPMI interface simply open your web browser to https://<IPMIAddress> Default logon for the Supermicro servers is UserID = ADMIN Password = ADMIN
>
> If the IPMI Addresses haven't been configured their DHCP address will show up during the power on and posting.

Post-Configuration of the S2D Nodes

With the nodes now fully turned on we can connect the S2D nodes to complete their final configuration tasks. It normally takes less than 1 hour to complete the entire post configuration. You can further automate this entire process by using the Microsoft Deployment Toolkit (MDT) or SCCM. Our nodes were pre-configured with an evaluation build of Windows Server 2016 Data Center Edition trial.

At a high level the remaining tasks are as follows:

- Change the names of the HyperConverged nodes
- Join the S2D nodes to a Domain (this is required if the nodes will be clustered using Microsoft Windows Failover Cluster)
- Install the required Roles and Features (Hyper-V, Failover Clustering, Data Center Bridging)
- Enable Datacenter Bridging
- Configure the SET Team and Virtual Adapters
- Configure an IP Addresses for the Virtual Adapters
- Run all Windows Updates
- Build the Cluster
- Enable Storage Spaces Direct
- Present the Storage
- Test

> **Note:** To automate this process a S2D Node Configuration PowerShell script can be been created. A sample configuration of an 8 Node S2D Cluster has been included as part of this book in Appendix A. It can also be downloaded from http://www.github.com/dkawula

Chapter 5   Deploying Storage Spaces Direct (S2D)

Building a 2-Node S2D Cluster

The following steps will demonstrate how to build out a 2-Node S2D Cluster. We will take 2 of the nodes that were purchased as part of the above solution to demonstrate this. This configuration is ideal for Small Office / Home Offices (SOHO) or Remote Office / Branch Offices (ROBO)

Install Core Windows Roles and features

The base Windows Server Roles and features required for S2D are listed below:

- File Services
- Failover Clustering (including Management Tools)
- Hyper-V (Including Management Tools)

You can install these via the GUI or with PowerShell. For the purposes of this book we will only be showing the configuration via PowerShell.

```
Install-WindowsFeature -Name File-Services
Install-WindowsFeature -Name Failover-Clustering -IncludeManagementTools
Install-WindowsFeature -Name Hyper-V -IncludeAllSubFeature -IncludeManagementTools -Restart
```

You can complete the Installation of the core roles on the remaining nodes by using the following PowerShell script.

```
Invoke-Command -ComputerName S2DNode2 -ScriptBlock {

Install-WindowsFeature -Name File-Services
Install-WindowsFeature -Name Failover-Clustering -IncludeManagementTools
Install-WindowsFeature -Name Hyper-V -IncludeAllSubFeature -IncludeManagementTools -Restart
}
```

Configuring Datacenter Bridging

The following Windows PowerShell script provides an example of how to enable and configure DCB for SMB Direct on S2DNode1:

```
#
# Turn on DCB
Install-WindowsFeature Data-Center-Bridging
#
# Set a policy for SMB-Direct
New-NetQosPolicy "SMB" -NetDirectPortMatchCondition 445 -PriorityValue8021Action 3
#
# Turn on Flow Control for SMB
Enable-NetQosFlowControl  -Priority 3
#
# Make sure flow control is off for other traffic
Disable-NetQosFlowControl  -Priority 0,1,2,4,5,6,7
#
# Apply policy to the target adapters
Enable-NetAdapterQos  -Name "Ethernet 1", "Ethernet 2"
#
# Give SMB Direct 30% of the bandwidth minimum
New-NetQosTrafficClass "SMB"  -Priority 3  -BandwidthPercentage 30  -Algorithm ETS
```

You can complete the installation of the DataCenter Bridging on the remaining nodes by running the following PowerShell command.

```
Invoke-Command -ComputerName S2DNode2 -ScriptBlock {
#
# Turn on DCB
Install-WindowsFeature Data-Center-Bridging
#
# Set a policy for SMB-Direct
New-NetQosPolicy "SMB" -NetDirectPortMatchCondition 445 -PriorityValue8021Action 3
#
# Turn on Flow Control for SMB
Enable-NetQosFlowControl  -Priority 3
#
# Make sure flow control is off for other traffic
Disable-NetQosFlowControl  -Priority 0,1,2,4,5,6,7
#
# Apply policy to the target adapters
Enable-NetAdapterQos  -Name "Ethernet","Ethernet 2"
#
# Give SMB Direct 30% of the bandwidth minimum
New-NetQosTrafficClass "SMB"  -Priority 3  -BandwidthPercentage 30  -Algorithm ETS
}
```

Chapter 5   Deploying Storage Spaces Direct (S2D)

Configuring the SET Team

A switch-embedded team must be created at the time the Hyper-V switch is created. When creating the Hyper-V switch using the **New-VMSwitch** PowerShell cmdlet, the **"EnableEmbeddedTeaming"** option must be selected.

Below is a screen shot of the network adapter configuration prior to building out the networking stack.

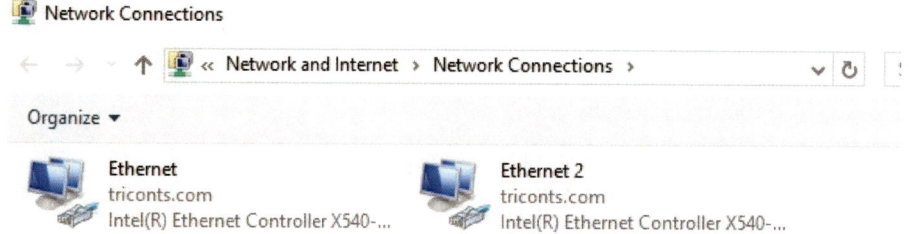

Figure 41 – Base Networking Configuration

Note: Although the configurations will appear to work on our Intel X540 10 GbE onboard network adapters. The RDMA Configurations and SMB Direct will not work. You must ensure that you purchase a supported network adapter for your configuration. RDMA over Converged Ethernet is what you want to look for and we personally recommend the: ConnectX®-3 Pro EN Single/Dual-Port Adapters 10/40/56GbE Adapters w/ PCI Express 3.0. More information can be found at Mellanox's website:
http://www.mellanox.com/page/products_dyn?product_family=162&mtag=connectx_3_pro_en_card

For the purpose of this book we decided to show the screenshots without the Mellanox cards and the configurations will work either way. You just won't get any benefits from RDMA in this config. We saw reasonable performance in our test lab and were waiting for new hardware at the time of writing the volume. In future versions, the goal is to have a more robust lab with multiple solutions.

To build the SET Team you can run the following PowerShell command

```
New-VMSwitch -Name TeamedvSwitch -NetAdapterName "Ethernet","Ethernet 2" -EnableEmbeddedTeaming $true
```

Chapter 5 Deploying Storage Spaces Direct (S2D)

You can complete the installation of the SET Team on the remaining nodes by running the following PowerShell command.

```
Invoke-Command -ComputerName S2DNode2 -ScriptBlock {

New-VMSwitch -Name TeamedvSwitch -NetAdapterName "Ethernet","Ethernet 2" -EnableEmbeddedTeaming $true

}
```

The result of the creation of the new SET Team looks like this in the Networking Control Panel.

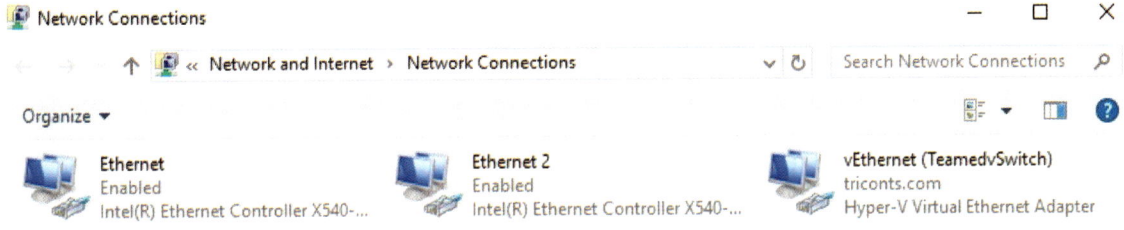

Figure 42 – SET Team created

Note: Remember that all configurations of the SET Teams are done through SCVMM or PowerShell. When you look at Server Manager you will see that NIC Teaming is disabled because this is only a view for LBFO Teaming.

Creating RDMA Enabled Virtual Adapters

Now that a SET Team has been created we need to create the RDMA enabled Virtual Adapters. This is what S2D will use its core network communications.

Below is a screen shot of the Network Control Panel after the new RDMA Virtual Adapters have been added.

109

Chapter 5   Deploying Storage Spaces Direct (S2D)

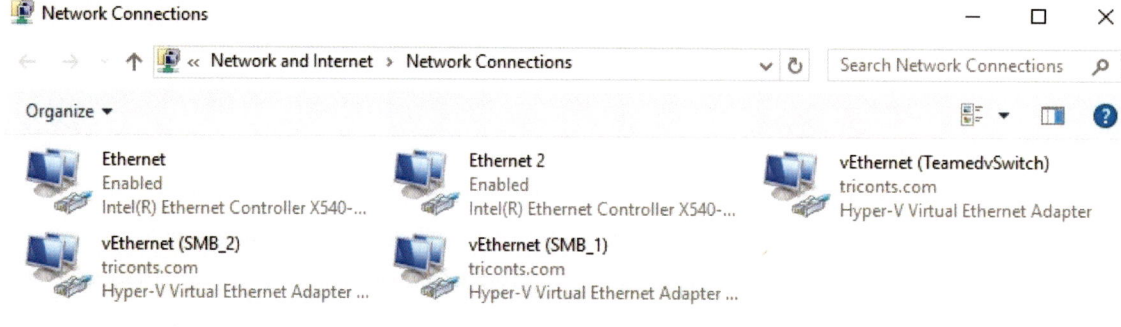

Figure 43 – RDMA Virtual Adapters Created

```
Add-VMNetworkAdapter -SwitchName TeamedvSwitch -Name SMB_1 -managementOS
Add-VMNetworkAdapter -SwitchName TeamedvSwitch -Name SMB_2 -managementOS
Enable-NetAdapterRDMA "vEthernet (SMB_1)","vEthernet (SMB_2)"
```

You can complete the installation of the RDMA enabled Virtual Adapters on the remaining nodes by running the following PowerShell command.

```
Invoke-Command -ComputerName S2DNode2 -ScriptBlock {

Add-VMNetworkAdapter -SwitchName TeamedvSwitch -Name SMB_1 -managementOS
Add-VMNetworkAdapter -SwitchName TeamedvSwitch -Name SMB_2 -managementOS
Enable-NetAdapterRDMA "vEthernet (SMB_1)","vEthernet (SMB_2)"

}
```

Verifying RDMA Enabled Virtual Adapters

To verify that the RDMA Enabled Virtual Adapters have been created properly you can run the following PowerShell command.   The below PowerShell commands will allow us to see if the configurations have been enabled or not on our Virtual Network Adapters.

```
Get-NetOffloadGlobalSetting | select networkdirect
Get-NetAdapterRdma
Get-NetAdapterHardwareInfo
```

Creating Virtual Adapters for Live Migration and Cluster Heartbeat

Now that we have RDMA enabled on our adapters for S2D we can create two more Virtual Adapters that will be dedicated for Live Migration and Cluster Heartbeat traffic.

To do this we can run the following PowerShell command.

```
Add-VMNetworkAdapter -SwitchName TeamedvSwitch -Name LM -managementOS
Add-VMNetworkAdapter -SwitchName TeamedvSwitch -Name HB -managementOS
```

You can complete the installation of the Live Migration and Cluster Heartbeat Virtual Adapters on the remaining nodes by running the following PowerShell command.

```
Invoke-Command -ComputerName S2DNode2 -ScriptBlock {

Add-VMNetworkAdapter -SwitchName TeamedvSwitch -Name LM -managementOS
Add-VMNetworkAdapter -SwitchName TeamedvSwitch -Name HB -managementOS

}
```

Configuring the IP Addresses for the S2D Nodes

All of the tasks above could be scripted or manually performed. IP Addresses that will be used for the S2D Cluster nodes are in the following table:

Host	SMB_1	SMB_2	LM	HB
S2DNODE1	10.10.199.1/16	10.11.0.1/24	10.12.0.1/24	10.13.0.1/24
S2DNODE2	10.10.199.2/16	10.11.0.2/24	10.12.0.2/24	10.13.0.2/24

To Configure S2D Nodes 1 and 2 the following PowerShell script was executed:

```
#Configure S2DNode1

New-NetIPAddress -IPAddress 10.10.199.1 -PrefixLength 16 -InterfaceAlias "vEthernet (SMB_1)" -DefaultGateway 10.10.0.254
Set-DnsClientServerAddress -InterfaceAlias "vEthernet (SMB_1)" -ServerAddresses 10.10.1.252
New-NetIPAddress -IPAddress 10.11.0.1 -PrefixLength 24 -InterfaceAlias "vEthernet (SMB_2)"
New-NetIPAddress -IPAddress 10.12.0.1 -PrefixLength 24 -InterfaceAlias "vEthernet (HB)"
New-NetIPAddress -IPAddress 10.13.0.1 -PrefixLength 24 -InterfaceAlias "vEthernet (LM)"

#Configure S2DNode2

Invoke-Command -ComputerName S2DNode2 -ScriptBlock {

New-NetIPAddress -IPAddress 10.10.199.2 -PrefixLength 16 -InterfaceAlias "vEthernet (SMB_1)" -DefaultGateway 10.10.0.254
Set-DnsClientServerAddress -InterfaceAlias "vEthernet (SMB_1)" -ServerAddresses 10.10.1.252
New-NetIPAddress -IPAddress 10.11.0.2 -PrefixLength 24 -InterfaceAlias "vEthernet (SMB_2)"
New-NetIPAddress -IPAddress 10.12.0.2 -PrefixLength 24 -InterfaceAlias "vEthernet (HB)"
New-NetIPAddress -IPAddress 10.13.0.2 -PrefixLength 24 -InterfaceAlias "vEthernet (LM)"

}
```

Chapter 5 Deploying Storage Spaces Direct (S2D)

Download and Install all Windows Updates

It is critical that all nodes of the S2D Cluster be updated prior to building the cluster. You should also check for any applicable hotfixes. This is a critical setup as many updates and hotfixes may have been released since your base OS Build or Gold Image was created.

Validate the Failover Cluster

Before creating the failover cluster, it is important to validate the components. Per Microsoft in order to have a supported cluster you must pass all of the Cluster Validation tests that are provided by Windows Server 2016.

To test the cluster via PowerShell run the following command.

```
Test-Cluster -Node S2DNode1,S2DNode2 -Include "Storage Spaces Direct", "Inventory", "System Configuration", "Network"
```

> **Note**: Once the tests have been completed you can view the results by checking the c:\windows\cluster\reports folder

You can see the output of the Failover Cluster Validation tests below. Ensure that you carefully review any or all of the warnings or errors prior to proceeding.

Chapter 5   Deploying Storage Spaces Direct (S2D)

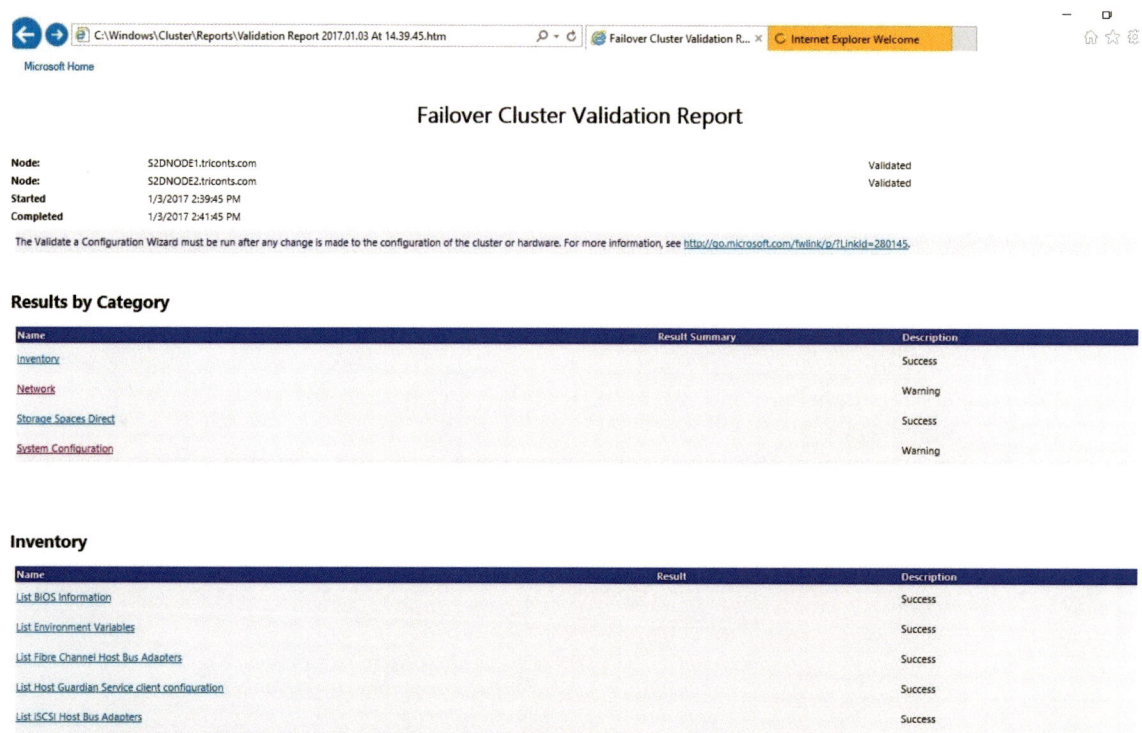

Figure 44 - Failover Cluster Validation Tests

Build the S2D Failover Cluster

Once the Failover Cluster Validation tests have passed you can now build the S2D Cluster. We will do this with the following one line PowerShell command.

```
New-Cluster -Name S2DCluster -Node S2DNode1,S2DNode2 -NoStorage -StaticAddress 10.10.199.20
```

In our example, we have given the Failover Cluster an IP Address of 10.10.199.20.

Validate the Cluster prior to Configuring Storage Spaces Direct (S2D)

It is important to run a few validation tests prior to enabling S2D. This can be done by running the following PowerShell commands.

```
Get-StorageSubSystem
```

```
PS C:\Windows\system32> Get-StorageSubSystem

FriendlyName                               HealthStatus OperationalStatus
------------                               ------------ -----------------
Windows Storage on S2DNODE1                Healthy      OK
Clustered Windows Storage on S2DCluster    Healthy      OK
```

Figure 45 – Get-StorageSubSystem View

You want to ensure that the OperationalStatus is OK.

```
Get-PhysicalDisk
```

```
PS C:\Windows\system32> Get-PhysicalDisk

FriendlyName         SerialNumber         CanPool OperationalStatus HealthStatus Usage            Size
------------         ------------         ------- ----------------- ------------ -----            ----
SATA SSD             96D707451524000028127 False  OK                Healthy      Auto-Select  59.63 GB
ATA Samsung SSD 840  S12SNEAD309432R      True    OK                Healthy      Auto-Select 476.94 GB
ATA ST1000LM014-1EJ1 W3802K9F             True    OK                Healthy      Auto-Select 931.51 GB
ATA ST1000LM014-1EJ1 W38064C6             True    OK                Healthy      Auto-Select 931.51 GB
ATA Samsung SSD 840  S12SNEAD309423E      True    OK                Healthy      Auto-Select 476.94 GB
```

Figure 46 – Get-PhysicalDisk View

You want to ensure that all of the disks that are participating in the S2D Cluster have a value of CanPool = True and OperationalStatus = OK.

If you have issues with your disks here it is likely that they have existing data on them. You can simply clean the disks and try again to fix this issue.

Enable Storage Spaces Direct (S2D)

Microsoft has made it extremely easy to enable Storage Spaces Direct in Windows Server 2016. In the RTM Build if you just run:

Chapter 5   Deploying Storage Spaces Direct (S2D)

```
Enable-ClusterStorageSpacesDirect -PoolFriendlyName S2DPool -confirm:$False
```

It will auto-provision the storage that will participate in the S2D Cluster. You can choose to do a manual configuration if you want. However, for the purpose of this chapter we have opted for the automatic configuration.

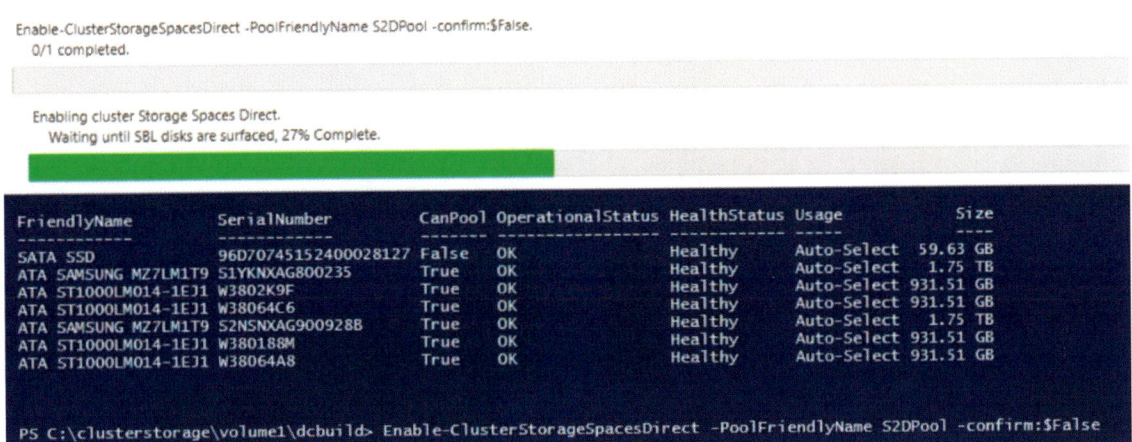

Figure 47 – Enable-ClusterStorageSpacesDirect in action

Note: All of the configuration reports are stored in C:\Windows\Cluster\Reports. The S2D Reports are stored with a pre-fix of Enable-ClusterS2D.

117

Provision Storage Virtual Disks (CSV)

As we are in only a 2 node S2D configuration we cannot take advantage of the Multi-Resilient volumes as described in Chapter 2 of this book. We are left with limited choices that include only a 2-way Mirror for protection.

The PowerShell command below will create a Virtual Disk called Mirror using the CSV File System and be formatted using ReFS. It will have a maximum size of 200 TB in this configuration.

```
New-Volume -StoragePoolFriendlyName S2DPool -FriendlyName Mirror -FileSystem CSVFS_REFS -Size 200GB -PhysicalDiskRedundancy 1
```

> **Note:** Remember that it is extremely important to understand that once you have created a Virtual Disk with it's resiliency settings it cannot be changed. It needs to be migrated to a different volume with different resiliency settings. In the case of Hyper-V this can be done by using Storage Live Migration in the same way that you would move data from a Lun to Lun.

Here we can see the newly presented Virtual Disk in Failover Cluster Manager.

Chapter 5   Deploying Storage Spaces Direct (S2D)

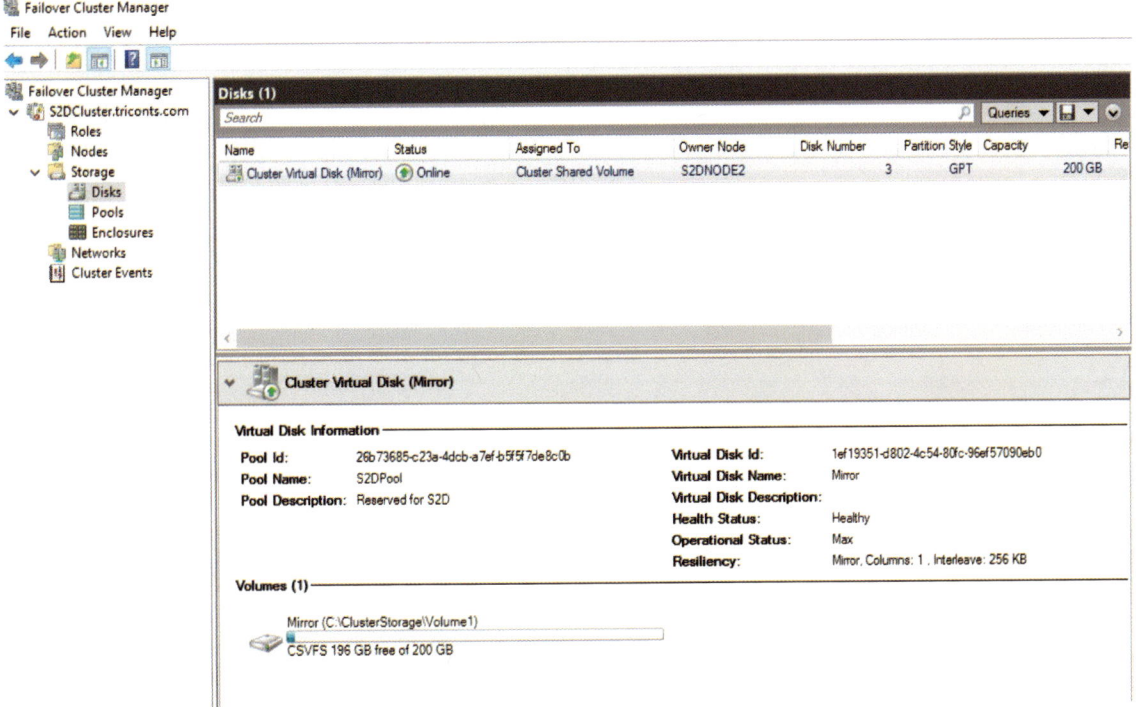

Figure 47 – Failover Cluster Manager view of S2D Volumes

As you can see below the newly created volume shows up as C:\ClusterStoreage\Volume1.

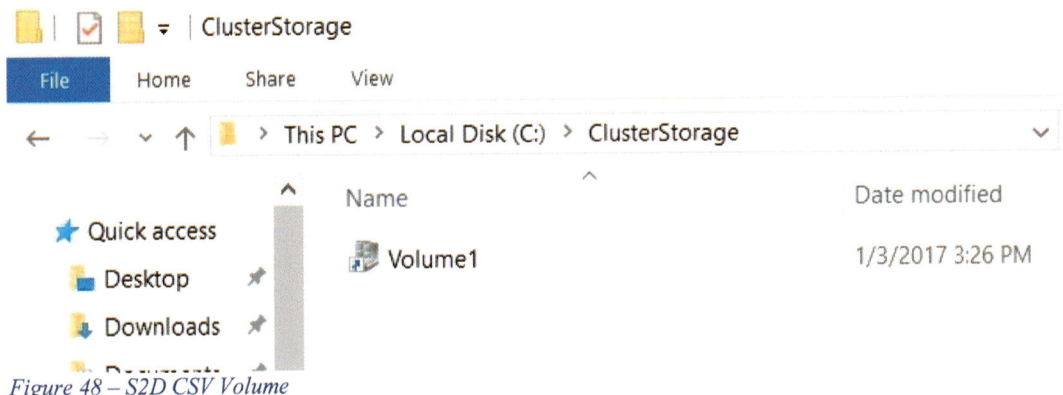

Figure 48 – S2D CSV Volume

Viewing S2D Volume info with Show Pretty Volume

This was a great script authored by Cosmos Darwin Storage PM at Microsoft. It will return a pretty little output from your newly minted S2D Cluster.

Here is the PowerShell Function he wrote:

```powershell
# Written by Cosmos Darwin, PM
# Copyright (C) 2016 Microsoft Corporation
# MIT License
# 8/2016

Function ConvertTo-PrettyCapacity {
    <#
    .SYNOPSIS
    Convert raw bytes into prettier capacity strings.

    .DESCRIPTION
    Takes an integer of bytes, converts to the largest unit (kilo-, mega-, giga-, tera-) that will result in at least 1.0, rounds to given precision, and appends standard unit symbol.

    .PARAMETER Bytes
    The capacity in bytes.

    .PARAMETER RoundTo
    The number of decimal places for rounding, after conversion.
    #>

    Param (
        [Parameter(
            Mandatory=$True,
            ValueFromPipeline=$True
            )
        ]
        [Int64]$Bytes,
        [Int64]$RoundTo = 0 # Default
    )

    If ($Bytes -Gt 0) {
        $Base = 1024 # To Match PowerShell
        $Labels = ("bytes", "KB", "MB", "GB", "TB", "PB", "EB", "ZB", "YB") # Blame Snover
        $Order = [Math]::Floor( [Math]::Log($Bytes, $Base) )
        $Rounded = [Math]::Round($Bytes/( [Math]::Pow($Base, $Order) ), $RoundTo)
        [String]($Rounded) + $Labels[$Order]
    }
    Else {
        0
    }
    Return
}

Function ConvertTo-PrettyPercentage {
    <#
    .SYNOPSIS
    Convert (numerator, denominator) into prettier percentage strings.
```

```powershell
        .DESCRIPTION
        Takes two integers, divides the former by the latter, multiplies by 100,
rounds to given precision, and appends "%".

        .PARAMETER Numerator
        Really?

        .PARAMETER Denominator
        C'mon.

        .PARAMETER RoundTo
        The number of decimal places for rounding.
    #>

    Param (
        [Parameter(Mandatory=$True)]
            [Int64]$Numerator,
        [Parameter(Mandatory=$True)]
            [Int64]$Denominator,
        [Int64]$RoundTo = 0 # Default
    )

    If ($Denominator -Ne 0) { # Cannot Divide by Zero
        $Fraction = $Numerator/$Denominator
        $Percentage = $Fraction * 100
        $Rounded = [Math]::Round($Percentage, $RoundTo)
        [String]($Rounded) + "%"
    }
    Else {
        0
    }
    Return
}

### SCRIPT... ###

$Output = @()

# Query Cluster Volumes
$Volumes = Get-StorageSubSystem Cluster* | Get-Volume

ForEach ($Volume in $Volumes) {

    # Get MSFT_Volume Properties
    $Label = $Volume.FileSystemLabel
    $Capacity = $Volume.Size | ConvertTo-PrettyCapacity
    $Used = ConvertTo-PrettyPercentage ($Volume.Size - $Volume.SizeRemaining) $Volume.Size

    If ($Volume.FileSystemType -Like "*ReFS") {
        $Filesystem = "ReFS"
    }
    ElseIf ($Volume.FileSystemType -Like "*NTFS") {
        $Filesystem = "NTFS"
    }

    # Follow Associations
    $Partition  = $Volume    | Get-Partition
    $Disk       = $Partition | Get-Disk
    $VirtualDisk = $Disk     | Get-VirtualDisk

    # Get MSFT_VirtualDisk Properties
    $Footprint = $VirtualDisk.FootprintOnPool | ConvertTo-PrettyCapacity
```

```powershell
    $Efficiency = ConvertTo-PrettyPercentage $VirtualDisk.Size $VirtualDisk.FootprintOnPool

    # Follow Associations
    $Tiers = $VirtualDisk | Get-StorageTier

    # Get MSFT_VirtualDisk or MSFT_StorageTier Properties...

    If ($Tiers.Length -Lt 2) {

        If ($Tiers.Length -Eq 0) {
            $ReadFrom = $VirtualDisk # No Tiers
        }
        Else {
            $ReadFrom = $Tiers[0] # First/Only Tier
        }

        If ($ReadFrom.ResiliencySettingName -Eq "Mirror") {
            # Mirror
            If ($ReadFrom.PhysicalDiskRedundancy -Eq 1) { $Resiliency = "2-way Mirror" }
            If ($ReadFrom.PhysicalDiskRedundancy -Eq 2) { $Resiliency = "3-way Mirror" }

            $SizeMirror = $ReadFrom.Size | ConvertTo-PrettyCapacity
            $SizeParity = [string](0)
        }
        ElseIf ($ReadFrom.ResiliencySettingName -Eq "Parity") {
            # Parity
            If ($ReadFrom.PhysicalDiskRedundancy -Eq 1) { $Resiliency = "Single Parity" }
            If ($ReadFrom.PhysicalDiskRedundancy -Eq 2) { $Resiliency = "Dual Parity" }

            $SizeParity = $ReadFrom.Size | ConvertTo-PrettyCapacity
            $SizeMirror = [string](0)
        }
        Else {
            Write-Host -ForegroundColor Red "What have you done?!"
        }
    }

    ElseIf ($Tiers.Length -Eq 2) { # Two Tiers

        # Mixed / Multi- / Hybrid
        $Resiliency = "Mix"

        ForEach ($Tier in $Tiers) {
            If ($Tier.ResiliencySettingName -Eq "Mirror") {
                # Mirror Tier
                $SizeMirror = $Tier.Size | ConvertTo-PrettyCapacity
                If ($Tier.PhysicalDiskRedundancy -Eq 1) { $Resiliency += " (2-Way" }
                If ($Tier.PhysicalDiskRedundancy -Eq 2) { $Resiliency += " (3-Way" }
            }
        }
        ForEach ($Tier in $Tiers) {
            If ($Tier.ResiliencySettingName -Eq "Parity") {
                # Parity Tier
                $SizeParity = $Tier.Size | ConvertTo-PrettyCapacity
                If ($Tier.PhysicalDiskRedundancy -Eq 1) { $Resiliency += " + Single)" }
                If ($Tier.PhysicalDiskRedundancy -Eq 2) { $Resiliency += " + Dual)" }
```

Chapter 5 Deploying Storage Spaces Direct (S2D)

```powershell
            }
        }
    }
    Else {
        Write-Host -ForegroundColor Red "What have you done?!"
    }

    # Pack

    $Output += [PSCustomObject]@{
        "Volume" = $Label
        "Filesystem" = $Filesystem
        "Capacity" = $Capacity
        "Used" = $Used
        "Resiliency" = $Resiliency
        "Size (Mirror)" = $SizeMirror
        "Size (Parity)" = $SizeParity
        "Footprint" = $Footprint
        "Efficiency" = $Efficiency
    }
}

$Output | Sort Efficiency, Volume | FT
```

And here is our Output running it:

Volume	Filesystem	Capacity	Used	Resiliency	Size (Mirror)	Size (Parity)	Footprint	Efficiency
Mirror	ReFS	200GB	3%	2-Way Mirror	200GB	0	400GB	50%

Figure 49 – Show-PrettyVolume.PS1

This script is a great way to see more detail on what has been configured in your S2D Cluster.

Here is a view of a larger system configured with multiple Virtual Disks and Resiliency Settings.

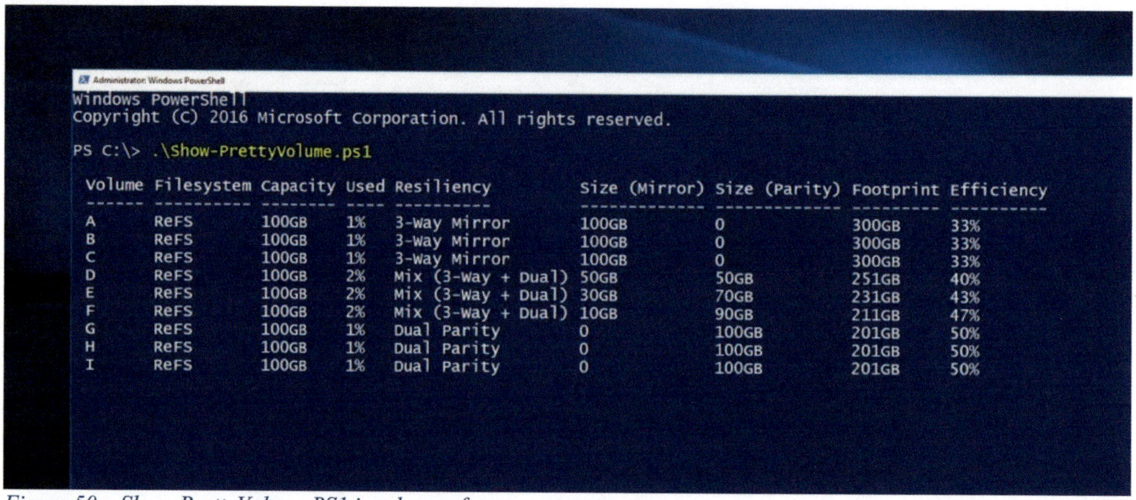

```
Windows PowerShell
Copyright (C) 2016 Microsoft Corporation. All rights reserved.

PS C:\> .\Show-PrettyVolume.ps1

Volume Filesystem Capacity Used Resiliency          Size (Mirror) Size (Parity) Footprint Efficiency
------ ---------- -------- ---- ----------          ------------- ------------- --------- ----------
A      ReFS       100GB    1%   3-Way Mirror        100GB         0             300GB     33%
B      ReFS       100GB    1%   3-Way Mirror        100GB         0             300GB     33%
C      ReFS       100GB    1%   3-Way Mirror        100GB         0             300GB     33%
D      ReFS       100GB    2%   Mix (3-Way + Dual)  50GB          50GB          251GB     40%
E      ReFS       100GB    2%   Mix (3-Way + Dual)  30GB          70GB          231GB     43%
F      ReFS       100GB    2%   Mix (3-Way + Dual)  10GB          90GB          211GB     47%
G      ReFS       100GB    1%   Dual Parity         0             100GB         201GB     50%
H      ReFS       100GB    1%   Dual Parity         0             100GB         201GB     50%
I      ReFS       100GB    1%   Dual Parity         0             100GB         201GB     50%
```

Figure 50 – Show-PrettyVolume.PS1 in a larger farm

Chapter 5   Deploying Storage Spaces Direct (S2D)

Expand the Virtual Disk

Now that we have such a small volume let's expand the Virtual Disk, doubling it's size to 400 GB. This can easily be done with this PowerShell Command below.

```
Get-VirtualDisk Mirror | Resize-VirtualDisk -Size 400GB
```

We don't have to worry about any Storage Tiers because this is only a 2-node configuration in our lab.

When we run the Show Pretty Volume script we can see that the Capacity of the Volume is still 200GB. This can also be verified with **Get-Volume** and indicates that we still have a bit of wrok to do.

```
Volume Filesystem Capacity Used Resiliency   Size (Mirror) Size (Parity) Footprint Efficiency
------ ---------- -------- ---- ----------   ------------- ------------- --------- ----------
Mirror ReFS       200GB    3%   2-Way Mirror 400GB         0             800GB     50%


PS C:\Windows\system32> Get-Volume

DriveLetter FileSystemLabel FileSystem DriveType HealthStatus OperationalStatus SizeRemaining      Size
----------- --------------- ---------- --------- ------------ ----------------- -------------      ----
            System Reserved NTFS       Fixed     Healthy      OK                   169.02 MB    500 MB
C                           NTFS       Fixed     Healthy      OK                    42.51 GB  59.14 GB
            Mirror          CSVFS      Fixed     Healthy      OK                   193.96 GB 199.81 GB
```

Figure 51 – Get-Volume Output

The goal was to increase this to the maximum size of 400 GB. This can be done by running the PowerShell command below.

```
$Cluster = "S2DCluster"
$VirtualDisks = Get-VirtualDisk Mirror
Get-VirtualDisk $VirtualDisks.FriendlyName | Get-Disk | Get-Partition | ? Type -EQ Basic | Resize-Partition -Size 400GB
```

This will resize the Volume using the newly created space that we have created in the Virtual disk. I often find that this illustration really depicts the flow of JBOD's, Virtual Disks, and Volumes.

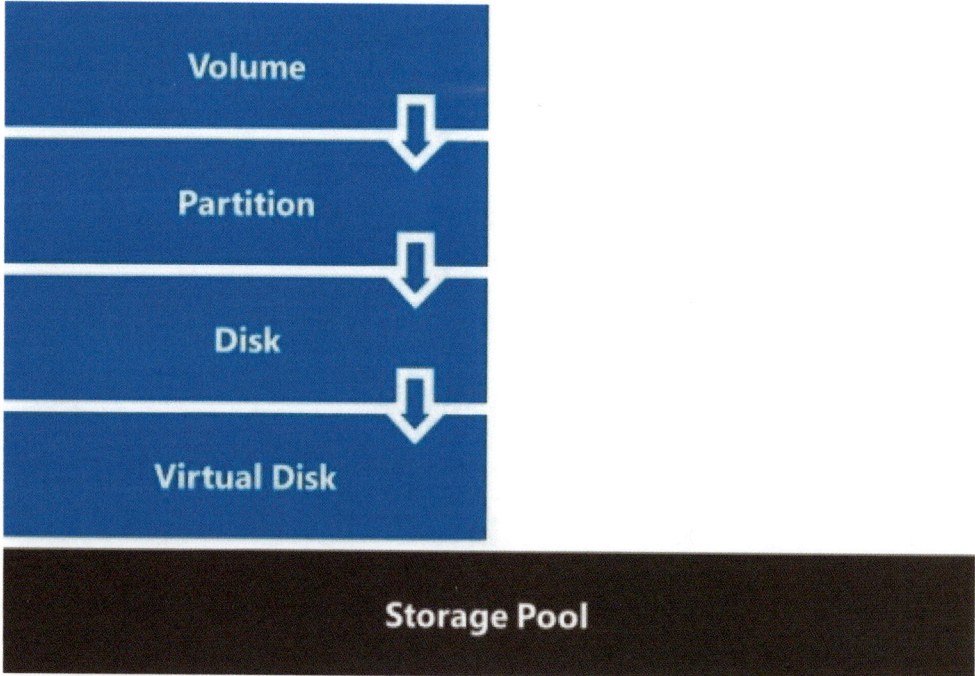

Figure 52 – Storage Architecture

Before being able to complete the task of expanding the Volume we first needed to add more space to the Virtual Disk. This is because we had maxed out the size during the initial provisioning process. We then had to Expand the Volume which is a similar process to expanding a LUN after it has had more space added in Windows through Disk Manager or Diskpart.

Here is what the finished product looks like in Failover Cluster Manager now that we have expanded our CSV Volume.

Chapter 5   Deploying Storage Spaces Direct (S2D)

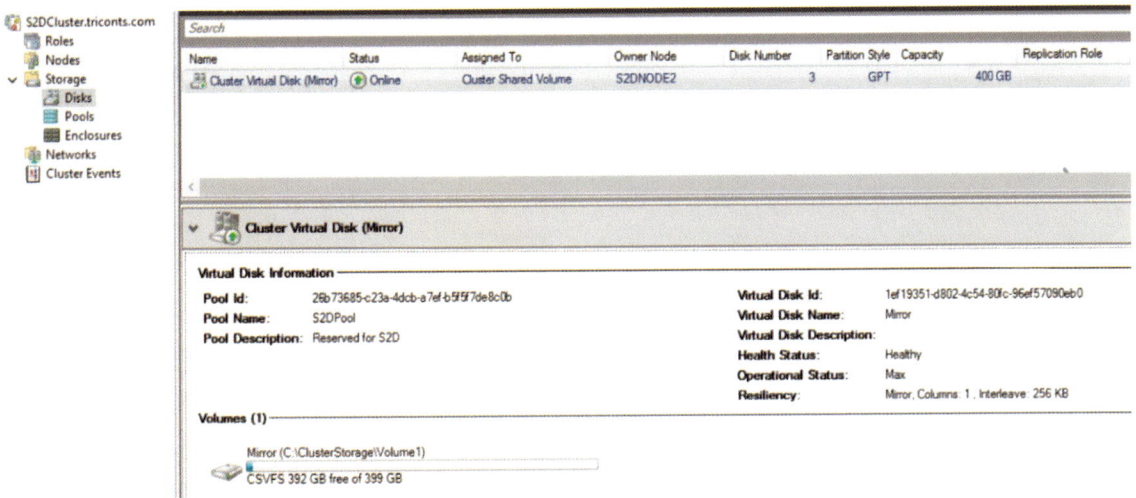

Figure 53 – Expanded S2D CSV Volume

Expand the Pool by adding more disks

So now the time has come to expand our S2D Pool. We can simply do this by adding more disks into our capacity tier.   We have acquired 2 additional 1 TB HDD Drives and now would like to get them added into the pool.   We have been told how easy this is so let's see it in action.

We now have the disks inserted and want to view their status by running the following PowerShell command.

`Get-physicaldisk`

The output isn't surprising as these have been reused disks from another farm and were likely not cleaned.   We can see that they have a health status of **Unknown** and an Operational Status of **Starting** as seen in the screen shot below.

127

Chapter 5   Deploying Storage Spaces Direct (S2D)

```
PS C:\Windows\system32> Get-physicaldisk

FriendlyName              SerialNumber           CanPool OperationalStatus HealthStatus Usage          Size
------------              ------------           ------- ----------------- ------------ -----          ----
SATA SSD                  96D70745152400028127   False   OK                Healthy      Auto-Select   59.63 GB
ATA Samsung SSD 840       S12SNEAD309432R        False   OK                Healthy      Journal      476.75 GB
ATA ST1000LM014-1EJ1      W3802K9F               False   OK                Healthy      Auto-Select   931.5 GB
ATA ST1000LM014-1EJ1      W38064C6               False   OK                Healthy      Auto-Select   931.5 GB
ATA Samsung SSD 840       S12SNEAD309423E        False   OK                Healthy      Journal      476.75 GB
ATA ST1000LM014-1EJ1      W380188M               False   Starting          Unknown      Unknown      931.51 GB
ATA ST1000LM014-1EJ1      W38064A8               False   Starting          Unknown      Unknown      931.51 GB
```

Figure 54 – Get-PhysicalDisk Output

This can be easily fixed by simply running the **Reset-PhysicalDisk** PowerShell command. Now in order to do this I have filtered the code below to look for a HealthStatus of unknown and reset all of the applicable disks.

```
$phydisk = (Get-Physicaldisk | Where-Object -FilterScript {$_.HealthStatus -Eq "Unknown"})

Reset-PhysicalDisk -FriendlyName $phydisk.FriendlyName

Get-physicaldisk
```

```
PS C:\Windows\system32>
Reset-PhysicalDisk -FriendlyName $phydisk.FriendlyName
PS C:\Windows\system32>
Get-physicaldisk

FriendlyName              SerialNumber           CanPool OperationalStatus HealthStatus Usage          Size
------------              ------------           ------- ----------------- ------------ -----          ----
SATA SSD                  96D70745152400028127   False   OK                Healthy      Auto-Select   59.63 GB
ATA Samsung SSD 840       S12SNEAD309432R        False   OK                Healthy      Journal      476.75 GB
ATA ST1000LM014-1EJ1      W3802K9F               False   OK                Healthy      Auto-Select   931.5 GB
ATA ST1000LM014-1EJ1      W38064C6               False   OK                Healthy      Auto-Select   931.5 GB
ATA Samsung SSD 840       S12SNEAD309423E        False   OK                Healthy      Journal      476.75 GB
ATA ST1000LM014-1EJ1      W380188M               True    OK                Healthy      Auto-Select  931.51 GB
ATA ST1000LM014-1EJ1      W38064A8               True    OK                Healthy      Auto-Select  931.51 GB
```

Figure 55 – Get-PhysicalDisk showing the new disks

After waiting only a few minutes we can see that the disk with a serial number of W380188M has already been added to the pool and S2D is automatically rebalancing across the new drives.

Chapter 5   Deploying Storage Spaces Direct (S2D)

```
PS C:\Windows\system32> Get-physicaldisk

FriendlyName              SerialNumber         CanPool OperationalStatus HealthStatus Usage           Size
------------              ------------         ------- ----------------- ------------ -----           ----
SATA SSD                  96D70745152400028127 False   OK                Healthy      Auto-Select  59.63 GB
ATA Samsung SSD 840       S12SNEAD309432R      False   OK                Healthy      Journal     476.75 GB
ATA ST1000LM014-1EJ1      W3802K9F             False   OK                Healthy      Auto-Select  931.5 GB
ATA ST1000LM014-1EJ1      W38064C6             False   OK                Healthy      Auto-Select  931.5 GB
ATA Samsung SSD 840       S12SNEAD309423E      False   OK                Healthy      Journal     476.75 GB
ATA ST1000LM014-1EJ1      W380188M             False   OK                Healthy      Auto-Select  931.5 GB
ATA ST1000LM014-1EJ1      W38064A8             True    OK                Healthy      Auto-Select 931.51 GB
```

Figure 56 – Get-PhysicalDisk Showing that the drives have automatically been added to the S2D Pool

We are able to check the progress of adding the new disks by running the following PowerShell command.

Get-StorageHealthAction

```
PS C:\Windows\system32> Get-StorageHealthAction

PercentComplete  State       Reason                                              PSComputerName
---------------  -----       ------                                              --------------
100              Succeeded   Restoring resiliency of the data.
100              Succeeded   Updating drive firmware across fault
                             domains.
100              Succeeded
100              Succeeded   Adding the physical disk to the storage
                             pool.
100              Succeeded   Setting the Cluster S2D Usage for the
                             subsystem.
```

Figure 57 – Get-StorageHealthAction Output

As you can see, it has already added the physical drive to the storage pool. During the writing of this book we were able to capture a screen shot of the rebalancing mid-flight from Failover Cluster Manager.

Chapter 5   Deploying Storage Spaces Direct (S2D)

PhysicalDisk5007 is the newly added disk and we can see the it has a used capacity of 65.3GB. This was actually taking space from Physical Disk5003 as it was decreasing from 400GB used.

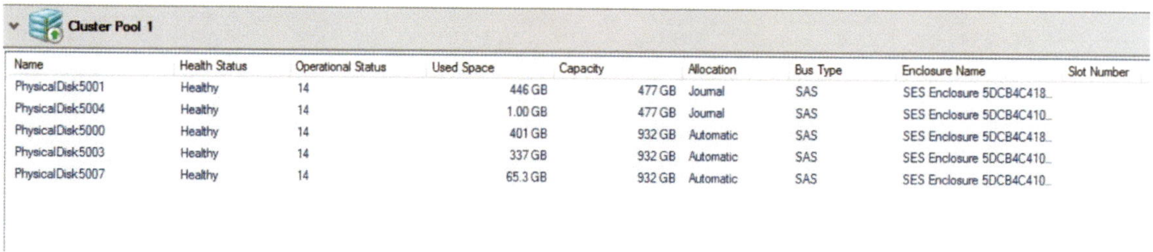

Name	Health Status	Operational Status	Used Space	Capacity	Allocation	Bus Type	Enclosure Name	Slot Number
PhysicalDisk5001	Healthy	14	446 GB	477 GB	Journal	SAS	SES Enclosure 5DCB4C418...	
PhysicalDisk5004	Healthy	14	1.00 GB	477 GB	Journal	SAS	SES Enclosure 5DCB4C410...	
PhysicalDisk5000	Healthy	14	401 GB	932 GB	Automatic	SAS	SES Enclosure 5DCB4C418...	
PhysicalDisk5003	Healthy	14	337 GB	932 GB	Automatic	SAS	SES Enclosure 5DCB4C410...	
PhysicalDisk5007	Healthy	14	65.3 GB	932 GB	Automatic	SAS	SES Enclosure 5DCB4C410...	

Figure 58 – Failover Cluster Manager showing the newly added disks

We can verify the percentage complete for the rebalancing by running the following PowerShell Command.

```
Get-StorageHealthAction
```

```
PS C:\Windows\system32>
Get-StorageHealthAction

PercentComplete   State        Reason                                            PSComputerName
---------------   -----        ------                                            --------------
100               Succeeded    Restoring resiliency of the data.
100               Succeeded    Updating drive firmware across fault
                               domains.
100               Succeeded
100               Succeeded    Adding the physical disk to the storage
                               pool.
48                Running      Rebalancing the storage pool.
100               Succeeded    Setting the Cluster S2D Usage for the
                               subsystem.
```

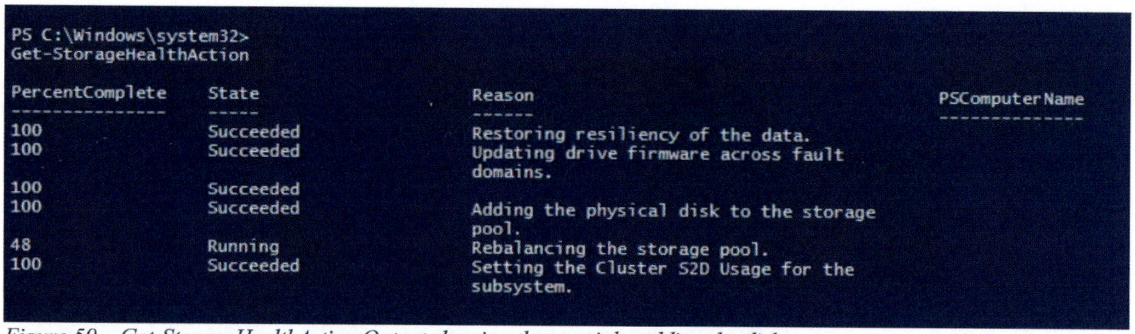

Figure 59 – Get-StorageHealthAction Output showing the new jobs adding the disks

Once this rebalancing process completes, the 2nd physical disk that we added will also be added to the Pool.

Now using Storage Spaces Direct we have configured our HyperConverged solution in less than an hour. Now it is off to stress testing in Chapter 6 with VMFleet.

Chapter 5 Deploying Storage Spaces Direct (S2D)

Chapter 6
Stress testing S2D using VMFleet

The VM Fleet is specifically adapted to performance analysis work, and allows an analyst to inject near real-time changes to the load as simply as editing and saving a script. This same mechanism can be used to create a simple demonstration environment that loops through a set of scripts.

This work is a prototype in progress, and presumes a hyper-converged deployment where the fleet VMs run on the same hardware as the Storage Spaces Direct cluster. There are certain assumptions that will require adaptation to run in generalized environments, which will be highlighted throughout the document.

> **Note**: The information in this chapter has come courtesy of the Microsoft Storage team via Technet.

Overview of VMFleet Scripts

The current scripting contains a few assumptions based on the environment it was developed in.

- that the VMs do not need external network connectivity
- that the central control point is within CSV
- location of central control point within CSV

The basic design is to create a fleet of VMs which autologin and launch a master control script which connects back to a known location in CSV, courtesy of a loopback through an internal vSwitch to their host. This script then launches the most-current load run script present, and monitors for updates and/or fleet pause requests.

Chapter 6 Stress testing S2D using VMFleet

> **Note:** Typically we have used tools like LoginVSI from LoginConsultants to perform similar tests in Citrix and RDS Farms. This tool is not a replacement for LoginVSI it is just a free tool for you to stress test your own farm. If you are building production farms make sure you get the right tools for the job.

SCRIPT	NOTES
LAUNCH-TEMPLATE.PS1	Per VM autologin script template: launches master.ps1, below, in a loop. ***Contains plaintext credentials when injected into the VMs.***
MASTER.PS1	Master control script for the VM. Copies in a toolset, runs load, monitors for master control and load run script updates, watches for the pause and sweep epochs.
CHECK-PAUSE.PS1	From the control console, checks how many pause acknowledgements have been received/host node. Enumerates non-paused VMs.
CLEAR-PAUSE.PS1	From the control console, clears a pause flag.
SET-PAUSE.PS1	From the control console, sets the pause flag.
INSTALL-VMFLEET.PS1	One-time script to install the vmfleet tools and create the control directory structure
CREATE-VMFLEET.PS1	Creates the per-node internal VM switches and deploys the VM Fleet VMs from a pre-created VHD master image.
SET-VMFLEET.PS1	Adjusts the number of VPs and memory size/type per VM.
DESTROY-VMFLEET.PS1	Removes all vmfleet VM content.
CHECK-VMFLEET.PS1	From the control console, checks the operational state of VMs hosted throughout the cluster.
START-VMFLEET.PS1	From the control console, launches all VMs currently in **OFF** state.
STOP-VMFLEET.PS1	From the control console, shuts down all VMs currently not in **OFF** state.
RUN.PS1	A standalone load run script. This specific form is simply an example, and can be anything.
RUN-DEMO-100R.PS1 RUN-DEMO-9010.PS1 RUN-DEMO-7030.PS1	These are example scripts used to set up performance demonstration environments. The demo.ps1 script, described below, causes the VM fleet to alternate between these.
RUN-SWEEPTEMPLATE.PS1	Template file for automated sweeps.
START-SWEEP.PS1	Control script for automated sweeps.
WATCH-CLUSTER.PS1	This is an example of text-console performance monitor tracking across a cluster. It displays the CSVFS IOP, bandwidth

	and latency counters, and aggregates them per-node and whole-cluster.
UPDATE-CSV.PS1	This script is used to manage the placement of tenant CSV volumes and VMs per a naming convention.
DEMO.PS1	An example script to run a looped demo load with Storage Quality of Service. Run alongside *Watch-Cluster*. This assumes a set of run-demo-*.ps1 scripts (such as those included above) and a specific set of QoS policies created ahead of time: SilverVM, GoldVM and PlatinumVM.
SET-STORAGEQOS.PS1	A wrapper for Set-VMHardDiskDrive, which takes a predefined Storage QoS Policy and applies it to all VMs within the hyperconverged cluster.

Master Control

To see the master control, load runner and pause in action, connect to one of the VMs. The color splash should help make the running operation self-describing. If an issue occurs, simply ^C back to the powershell prompt (note -noexit in the launch parameters) and debug/restart the launch script, or simply shut down and reboot the VM.

Building VMFleet

The VM Fleet operates on VMs installed across:

- a set of one or more CSV created per cluster node for its VMs, with virtual disks (and as a result, CSVs) named following the pattern of <node name>[-suffix].
- with tools located in a VD/CSV named "collect"
- These CSVs are mounted in C:\ClusterStorage per the friendly name. This convention simplifies a few tasks:
- moving CSVs within the cluster and back to their nominal owner node
- for a given host, finding its nominally owned CSV

This has proven effective in eliminating the need for additional configuration documentation, such as an XML description of the mappings. VMs are named following a similar pattern: vm-[-group/virtual disk suffix]-<nodename>-<number>

Creating the Cluster Shared Volumes (CSV) for the tests

The following fragment is an example of creating CSVs following the node naming convention, assuming that the Storage Spaces Direct pool is named per the default used by Enable-ClusterS2D. Any appropriate CSV filesystem type, size or resiliency can be used.

```
Get-ClusterNode |% {
    New-Volume -StoragePoolFriendlyName S2D* -FriendlyName $_ -FileSystem CSVFS_ReFS -Size 1TB
} New-Volume -StoragePoolFriendlyName S2D* -FriendlyName collect -FileSystem CSVFS_ReFS -Size 1TB
```

Install the VMFleet Scripts

Copy the VM Fleet scripts into a cluster node and run the install-vmfleet script. This will:
- set the well-named mountpoints in C:\ClusterStorage
- create the basic directory structure within C:\ClusterStorage\collect
- control : the location for the scripts
- control\tools : the location from which VMs will pick up additional tool content
- control\result : the location to which VMs will copy their load results

- copy the scripts into control
- add control to the current user's path
- set fleet pause (set-pause)

Create the VMFleet Golden Image

The VM fleet has been built focusing on the Server Core image for the guest VMs. The only requirement is that the administrator password has been set.

To construct the image, create a VM on a Server Core VHDX or install a Server Core VM using ISO media. Once installed, launch the VM and follow the prompts to specify the administrator password. This password will be specified later to the create-vmfleet script which deploys the VMs. Then tear down the VM – the resulting VHDX will be used.

It should be possible to use full SKUs. The most immediate change is that they will need to use shell startup items to run the launch script that is injected by the specializer. This mechanism is not used on Core since it lacks the shell.

Create the Fleet VMs

The **create-vmfleet** script provisions VMs for the fleet.

By default, a dynamic VHDX will be converted to a fixed VHDX before using it for provisioning. This eliminates certain warmup effects that would occur if the VHDX remained dynamic or if the VHDX was converted to a fixed VHDX at its destination. If there is a specific measurement or deployment goal, though, it is reasonable to deploy with dynamic/unseasoned content and drive through the warmup effects that that mode of operation implies.

The script performs the following steps. It is idempotent, i.e. it can be rerun if failures occur to complete the specified deployment.

- deploys one internal vmswitch per node with the IPv4 APIPA IP 169.254.1.1; this will be the connectivity for the VMs back through the host
- copies a gold/base VHD per VM
- instantiates a VM over that VHD
- instantiates a clustered VM role for the VM
- specializes the VM/VHD
    - sets up autologin of the administrative account
    - installs VM fleet launch scripting
    - creates a sample load file for DISKSPD

Chapter 6 Stress testing S2D using VMFleet

- o creates an identification file naming the VM (c:\vmspec.txt)

To prepare for deployment, provide access to the VHD prepared.

Create-vmfleet has the following switches:

- basevhd : the path to the prepared VHD
- vms : the number of vms per node per csv (group) to create
- group : specify an explicit group; else (default) it is inherited from the suffix of the CSV virtualdisk friendlyname, i.e.: <nodename>-<suffix>
- adminpass : password for the VM-local administrative user
- admin : (default: administrator) name of the VM-local administrative user
- connectpass : password for the user to establish the loopback connection to the host
- connectuser: name of the user to establish the loopback connection to the host
- stopafter : (not normally needed) used for triage, halts deployment at a specific step for each VM
- specialize : (not normally needed) specifies whether specialization should
    - o auto : (default) be done as each VM is deployed
    - o none : not be performed
    - o force : always be performed, even if the VM is already deployed
    - o fixedvhd: (not normally needed) if $false, allows the base VHD to be dynamic

Note: Specialization requires that the VM be offline. If the VM is online, the specialization process cannot mount the VHD to inject the content. The master.ps1 script and default load file is placed at C:\run in the VM VHDX.

If an alternate network configuration is desirable, update create-vmfleet and ensure master.ps1 is modified as needed so that the VMs can establish their loopback connection to their host to CSV.

The default VM sizing follows the defaults for the New-VM cmdlet. To set a specific VM sizing, use the **set-vmfleet** script. Its options follow the Set-VM cmdlet:

- ProcessorCount : VP count per VM
- MemoryStartupBytes : memory reserved at VM startup
- MemoryMaximumBytes : maximum memory per VM
- DynamicMemory : (default: no, i.e. StaticMemory) whether dynamic memory is enabled

The Azure A-series VM sizes provide a baseline for VM sizing.

Run the VM Fleet

At this point, the VM fleet should be ready for operation.

In addition to the pause/stop/start scripts, the basic control mechanism involves the VMs watching for an updated run*.ps1 script (note the wildcard) in the control directory. The master script checks every five seconds for pause or run script updates, so any changes should propagate in near real-time to the fleet.

Storage QoS

Storage Quality of Service is a new capability for Windows Server 2016. To use this with the VM Fleet, define one or more per-VM polices. Examples:

```
New-StorageQosPolicy -Name SilverVM -MaximumIops 500 -PolicyType Dedicated
New-StorageQosPolicy -Name GoldVM -MaximumIops 5000 -PolicyType Dedicated
New-StorageQosPolicy -Name PlatinumVM -MaximumIops 10000 -PolicyType Dedicated
```

Earlier versions of Windows Server 2016 Technical Previews used the policy type name MultiInstance instead of Dedicated. Both refer to a policy whose rate limit applies to each VM individually.

These names correspond to those used within the demo.ps1 demonstration script. They individually specify a range of 20x (500 – 10,000) IOP controls to put on the VMs. To then apply these policies to the VMs, use the set-storageqos.ps1 script.

> **Note:** If a dynamic VHDX is used as the base and it is promoted to a fixed VHDX, the expanded region is a sparse (but reserved) hole in the ReFS allocation map for the file. In order to avoid warmup effects of committing allocation for the hole, the load file in the VM VHDX should be pre-seasoned prior to use unless these warmup effects are the specific goal of any measurements. Large sequential IO is preferred for seasoning.

Automated Sweeps

As of version 0.4, VM Fleet has an initial set of mechanics for automated performance sweeps. This is based on an epoch ask/response similar to how pause works.

- master tracks a "go" epoch and listens for a "done" response from run scripts
- when "done" is received, master drops a done flag file indicating the "go" epoch
- start-sweep uses this interaction to step the fleet through a sequence of run scripts, ensuring that the fleet has successfully completed each step before moving to the next
    - generated off of run-sweeptemplate.ps1
    - place into run-sweep.ps1 for each step

With version 0.5, start-sweep now accepts all parameters on the command line:

- runtemplate: the template run script which will have substitutions applied to it to produce the run file for each step (default: c:\clusterstorage\collect\control\run-sweeptemplate.ps1)
- runfile: the name to use for the run file itself (default: c:\clusterstorage\collect\control\run-sweep.ps1)
- labeltemplate: the list of sweep parameters to append together to create unique result filenames (default: b, t, o, w, p, addspec – this will generally not need to be modified)
- pc: a list of performance counters to capture in the host (ex: "\Hyper-V Hypervisor Logical Processor(*)*")
- parameters corresponding to DISKSPD:
    - b: list of buffer sizes (KiB)
    - t: list of thread counts
    - o: list of outstanding IO counts
    - w: list of write ratios
    - p: list of patterns (random: r, sequential: s, sequential interlocked: si)
    - warm: duration of pre-measurement warmup (seconds)
    - d: duration of measured interval (seconds)
    - cool: duration of post-measurement cooldown (seconds)

o addspec: inserts an arbitrary string into the result file name, to distinguish multiple sweeps which vary external parameters not under start-sweep's control. For instance: CSV placement, VCPU counts, VM numbers, and so forth.

The combination of parameters specified as lists (btowp) results in the given number of variations being run. For instance, 4, 8, and 64 KiB buffer size and 0, 10, and 30% write ratios would result in 3 x 3 = 9 variations if all other parameters were specified with single values (1 thread, etc.).

If additional controls are needed on DISKSPD, or any other tooling, simply add corresponding parameters to start-sweep, modify how the [variableset] is populated and possibly extend the default label template. Look for this block to locate the code to modify:

```
###########################
###########################
## Modify from here down
###########################
```

The default sweep template will drop DISKSPD XML results into the collect\control\result folder, which must already exist. It is currently a flagged error if any VM indicates early completion of a step, so ensure that the result folder does not have pre-existing results.

CPU Target Sweeps

The CPU Target Sweep is the first higher order sweep using the sweep mechanics.

S2D, like many similar systems, will generally become CPU limited when doing small IOs. While the resulting absolute performance statements can be an exciting measure of system efficiency – 1-2 million IOPS or more! – they are not results which a realistic application (or set of VMs) could achieve since they would have little leftover CPU to drive the system.

This is where the CPU Target Sweep comes in. Using Storage QoS (see Section 5Error! Reference source not found.) and a simple linear extrapolation, it drives the system to a specific %CPU utilization over 100% 4KiB read and 90:10 and 70:30 r/w.

The script, sweep-cputarget, takes two parameters:

o outfile: name of the result tab-seperated-value file
o cputargets: list of specific %cpu targets (ex: 20, 40, 60)

CPU is targeted +/- 5%. In practice these should indeed be linearly related through 60%. Take care in extrapolating to high average CPU utilization since saturation introduces non-linear (limiting) effects.

The analyze-cputarget script produces a report containing linear fits $(y = a + bx)$ based on the output of the sweep:

Chapter 6 Stress testing S2D using VMFleet

- csvfile: name of the cputarget result file
- zerointercept: whether the equations should be forced to state average CPU = 0 implies IOPS = 0 (default: false)

The zero intercept option should be used with care. A non-zero constant usually results in a better fit in the middle ranges of CPU utilization most relevant here: 20% CPU for storage, 80% CPU for VMs/Applications, and the like.

In general, 15%-80% should be relatively well handled with a linear relationship, though it is your responsibility to understand these results and make sure they are applicable to your scenario & system.

Alternate sweeps – different r/w mixes, buffer sizes – can be done by editing sweep-cputarget.

Chapter 7

Deploying an 8 Node S2D Lab Using Hyper-V

Now that you have seen how to build a physical S2D Cluster. You are probably thinking that it would be nice to build your very own for testing and lab purposes. Well we have a nice little bonus for you as part of this book. We have authored a script that will build you a nice Hyper-V lab environment including the following servers:

- Domain Controller 1
- Domain Controller 2
- DHCP Server
- Management Server
- 8 S2D Nodes

All of the code has been constructed from a demo script that we first saw Ben Armstrong @VirtualPCGuy showcase for one of his demos. It is very easy to customize to build your own lab environment especially if you want to build a smaller farm.

Basically, all you need to do to run this is download an RTM copy of the Windows 2016 ISO and place it in the working directory.

For my example, we have used the following parameters for the script execution:

- $WorkingDir = C:\ClusterStorage\Volume1\DCBuild
- $Organization = MVPDays
- $Owner = Dave Kawula
- $TimeZone = Pacific Standard Time

- $AdminPassword = P@ssw0rd
- $DomainName = MVPDays.com
- $domainAdminPassword = P@ssw0rd
- $VirtualSwitchName = MVPDays_Vswitch
- $Subnet = 172.16.200.
- $ExtraLabFiles = C:\ClusterStorage\Volume1\DCBuild\Extralabfiles

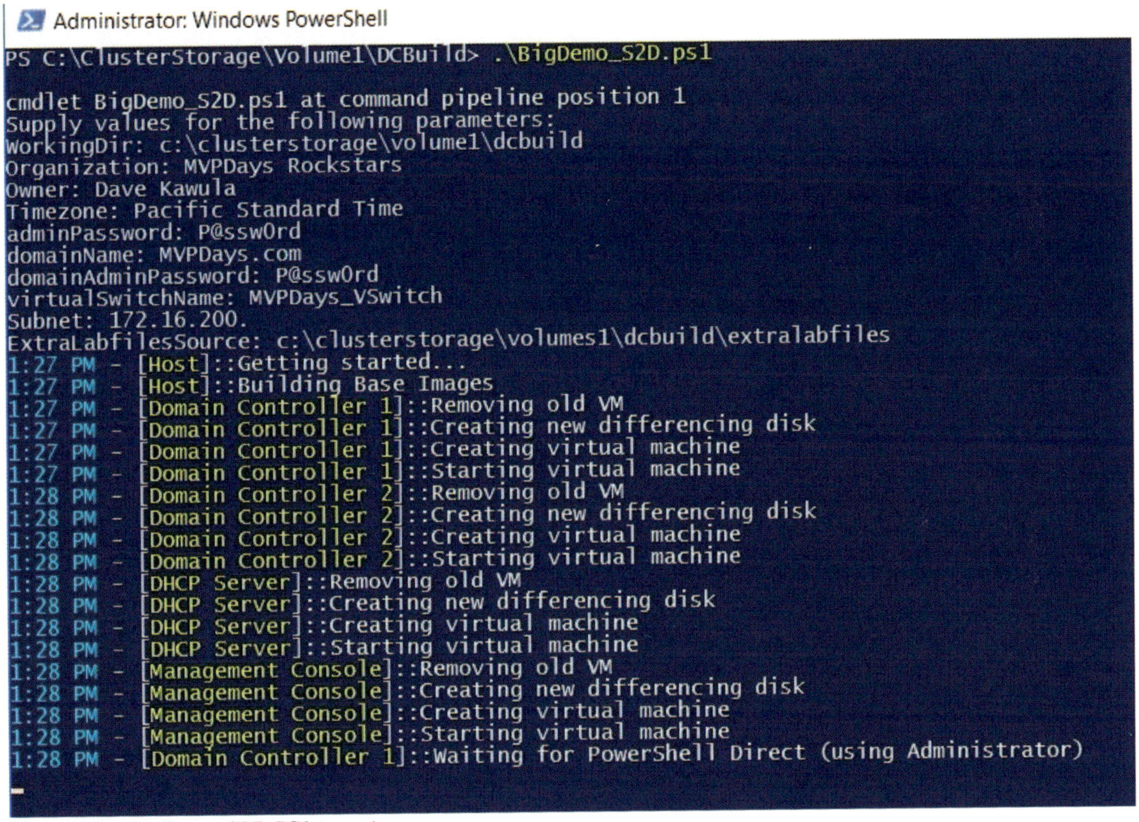

Figure 60 – BigDemo_S2D.PS1 in action

Once the Domain Controllers, DHCP, and Management Servers complete their build then the S2D Nodes will commence their build.

As mentioned, the process is completely automated with this script from the Creation of Active Director, DHCP Server, Management, and the full build of the S2D Cluster.

Chapter 7   Deploying an 8 Node S2D Lab Using Hyper-V

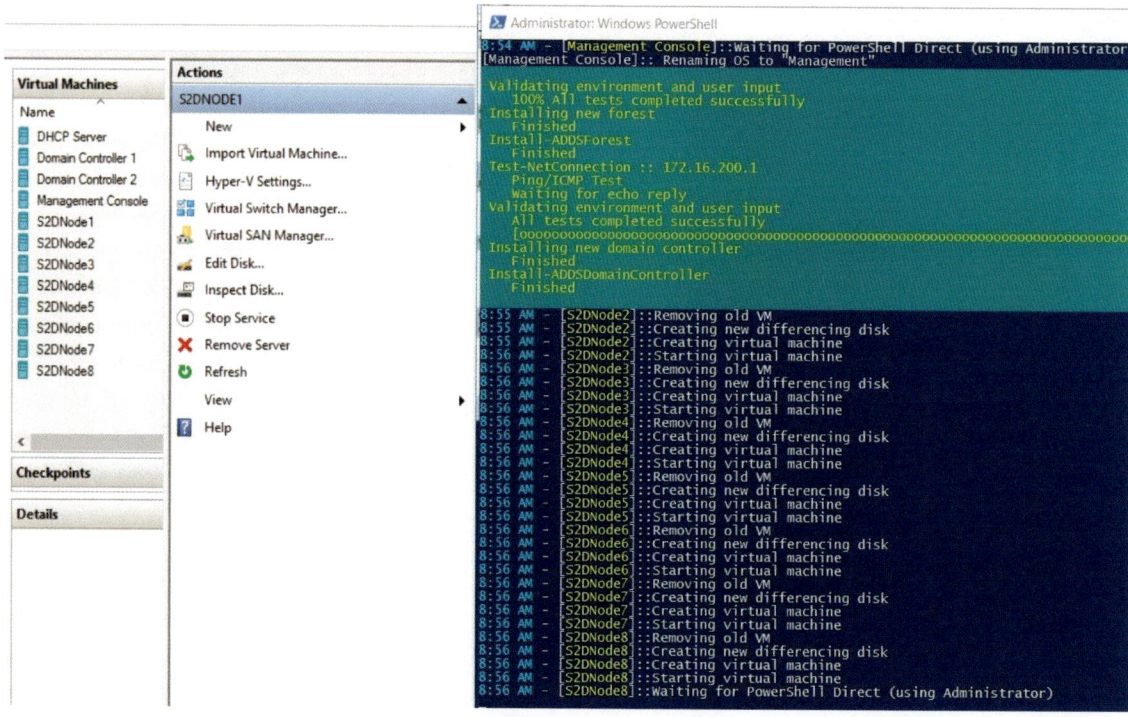

Figure 61 – BigDemo_S2D.PS1 building an 8 node S2D Lab

This script can be easily customized to add whatever number of S2D nodes you would like. It is hard coded right now for 8 S2D nodes in order to fit on most testing laptops.

Name	State	CPU Usage	Assigned Memory	Uptime	Status	Configurati...
DHCP Server	Running	0 %	4096 MB	00:27:30		8.0
Domain Controller 1	Running	0 %	4096 MB	00:34:16		8.0
Domain Controller 2	Running	0 %	4096 MB	00:23:21		8.0
Management Console	Running	0 %	4096 MB	00:21:31		8.0
S2DNode1	Running	0 %	4096 MB	00:12:59		8.0
S2DNode2	Running	0 %	4096 MB	00:07:58		8.0
S2DNode3	Running	0 %	4096 MB	00:03:01		8.0
S2DNode4	Running	1 %	4096 MB	00:01:14		8.0
S2DNode5	Running	0 %	4096 MB	00:19:01		8.0
S2DNode6	Running	0 %	4096 MB	00:18:53		8.0
S2DNode7	Running	0 %	4096 MB	00:18:41		8.0
S2DNode8	Running	0 %	4096 MB	00:18:37		8.0
S2DNode9	Running	0 %	4096 MB	00:18:25		8.0
S2DNode10	Running	0 %	4096 MB	00:18:20		8.0
S2DNode11	Running	0 %	4096 MB	00:18:11		8.0
S2DNode12	Running	0 %	4096 MB	00:18:07		8.0
S2DNode13	Running	0 %	4096 MB	00:18:03		8.0
S2DNode14	Running	0 %	4096 MB	00:17:59		8.0
S2DNode15	Running	0 %	4096 MB	00:17:55		8.0
S2DNode16	Running	0 %	4096 MB	00:17:53		8.0

Figure 62 – BigDemo_S2D.PS1 building a 16 node S2D Lab

Chapter 7 Deploying an 8 Node S2D Lab Using Hyper-V

In the script, we also attempt to emulate a production like environment so we have configured some teams.

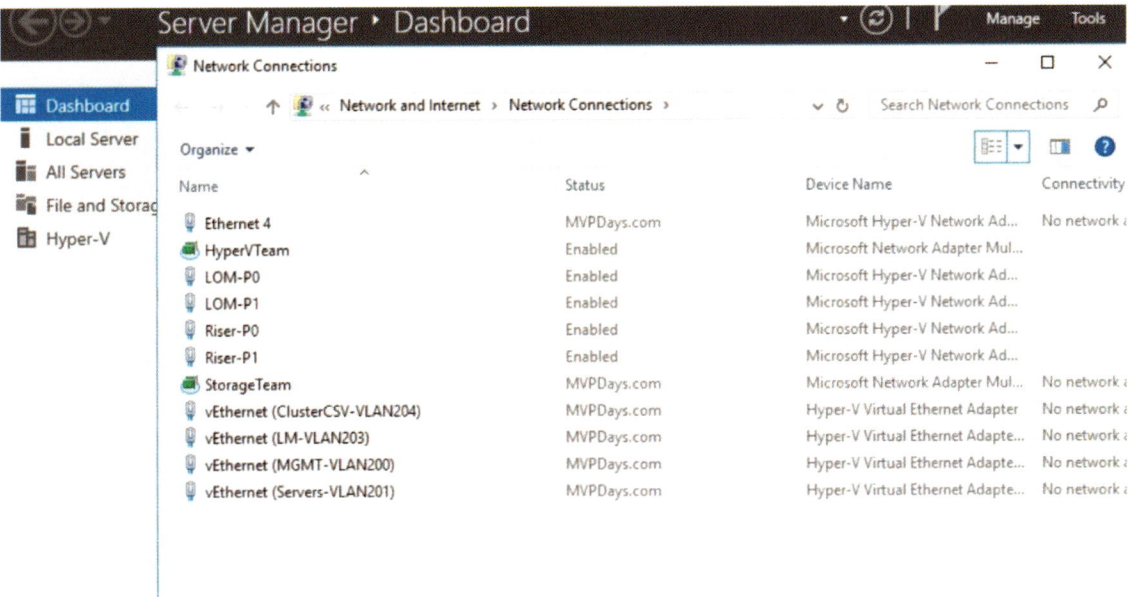

Figure 63 – BigDemo_S2D.PS1 in action showing Configuring the Network Stack of the S2D Nodes

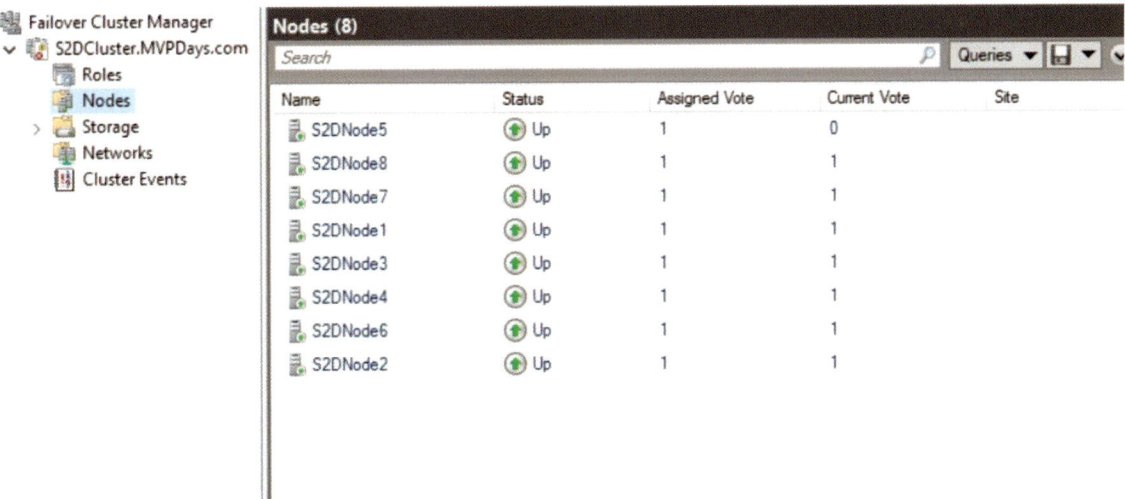

Figure 64 – BigDemo_S2D.PS1 in action showing Failover Cluster Manager with 8 of the S2D Nodes

To download the script, go to http://www.github.com/dkawula

Chapter 7 Deploying an 8 Node S2D Lab Using Hyper-V

The name of the script is called BigDemo_S2D.PS1

It has also been copied into Appendix A at the end of this book.

Chapter 8
Factory Reset of Storage Spaces Direct

There are a lot of objects that get created automatically when we configure Storage Spaces Direct. It can be handy when learning to re-start the lab configuration without having to rebuild your servers. The script in this chapter acts as a Factory Reset for Storage Spaces Direct.

There is a handy script up in the TechNet gallery that I use for this job called Clear-SDSConfig.PS1.

https://gallery.technet.microsoft.com/scriptcenter/Completely-Clearing-an-ab745947

> **Note:** *Huge word of caution this script will tear down everything you have built with a sledge hammer. You will have data loss and this should be used with caution.*

I know you can just download the script however, I felt it would be handy to read through all of the items that need to be cleaned up to start over.

Clear-SDSConfig.PS1

```
################################    WARNING    ################################
#                                                                             #
#                    ***    USE AT YOUR OWN RISK    ***                       #
#                    PERMANANT DATA LOSS WILL OCCUR                           #
#                                                                             #
# This script completely clears any existing Storage Spaces configuration     #
# and all data on EVERY non-system drive PERMANENTLY!                         #
#                                                                             #
# Notes:                                                                      #
#                                                                             #
#    If certain drives cannot be cleared and the reason given is              #
#    'Redundant Path' then MPIO may need to be installed and/or configured.   #
#                                                                             #
#    Power cycling the JBOD enclosures can also remove additional             #
#    errors encountered during the run.                                       #
#                                                                             #
#    Run cmdlet with Administrator rights.                                    #
#                                                                             #
################################    WARNING    ################################

################################    Change Log    ################################
#                                                                                #
```

```powershell
# 02/13/2014: Changed logic to remove SAS-connected boot/system disks      #
# 02/13/2014: Changed output for clearing disks and tracking runtime       #
# 04/07/2014: Corrected logic to deal boot and system drives               #
# 04/07/2014: Added logic to deal with non-core cluster objects            #
# 07/23/2015: Changes to better support Storage Spaces Direct              #
#                                                                          #
############################################################################

[CmdletBinding(SupportsShouldProcess=$true, ConfirmImpact="High")]
param()

if ($PSCmdlet.ShouldProcess("localhost","Clear Storage Spaces configuration and wipe disks"))
{
    Write-Host ""
    Write-Host Clearing existing Storage Spaces configuration and wiping disks...
    Write-Host ""

    $runStart = [DateTime]::Now

    # Install necessary tools if needed
    $toolsInstalled = $false
    if (!(Get-WindowsFeature -Name "RSAT-Clustering-PowerShell").Installed)
    {
        Write-Host Installing required tools... -ForegroundColor Cyan -NoNewline
        Install-WindowsFeature -Name "RSAT-Clustering-PowerShell"
        $toolsInstalled = $true
        Write-Host Done.
        Write-Host ""
    }

    # Remove any cluster objects if present
    Write-Host "Removing any cluster objects" -NoNewline -ForegroundColor Cyan
    Write-Host "..." -NoNewline

    foreach ($clusterGroup in (Get-ClusterGroup -ErrorAction SilentlyContinue -WarningAction SilentlyContinue))
    {
        if (!$clusterGroup.IsCoreGroup)
        {
            Remove-ClusterGroup -Name $clusterGroup.Name -Force:$true -RemoveResources:$true -ErrorAction SilentlyContinue
        }
    }

    Remove-Cluster -Force -CleanupAD -ErrorAction SilentlyContinue -WarningAction SilentlyContinue

    Write-Host "Done."

    $disks = Get-PhysicalDisk | Where-Object {($_.BusType -EQ "SAS") -or ($_.BusType -EQ "SATA")} # -or ($_.BusType -EQ "RAID")}

    Write-Host ""
    Write-Host "Removing any stale PRs" -NoNewline -ForegroundColor Cyan
    Write-Host "..." -NoNewline
    foreach ($disk in $disks)
    {
        Clear-ClusterDiskReservation -Disk $disk.DeviceId -Force -ErrorAction SilentlyContinue -WarningAction SilentlyContinue
    }
```

```powershell
    Write-Host "Done."

    Write-Host ""
    Write-Host "Updating the storage provider cache (x2)" -NoNewline -ForegroundColor Cyan
    Write-Host "..." -NoNewline
    Update-StorageProviderCache -DiscoveryLevel Full
    Start-Sleep 1
    Update-StorageProviderCache -DiscoveryLevel Full
    Write-Host "Done."

    # Remove virtual disks and storage pools
    Write-Host ""
    Write-Host "Removing Virtual Disks and Pools" -NoNewline -ForegroundColor Cyan
    Write-Host "..." -NoNewline
    $storagePools = Get-StoragePool | ? FriendlyName -NE "primordial"
    $storagePools | Set-StoragePool -IsReadOnly:$false
    Get-VirtualDisk | Set-VirtualDisk -IsManualAttach:$false
    Get-VirtualDisk | Remove-VirtualDisk -Confirm:$false
    $storagePools | Remove-StoragePool -Confirm:$false
    Write-Host "Done."
    Write-Host ""

    Write-Host "Updating the storage provider cache (x2)" -NoNewline -ForegroundColor Cyan
    Write-Host "..." -NoNewline
    Update-StorageProviderCache -DiscoveryLevel Full
    Start-Sleep 1
    Update-StorageProviderCache -DiscoveryLevel Full
    Write-Host "Done."
    Write-Host ""

    # Collect IDs of any system/boot disks
    $disks = Get-Disk
    $diskIdsToRemove = @()
    foreach ($disk in $disks)
    {
        if ($disk.IsBoot -or $disk.IsSystem)
        {
            $diskIdsToRemove += $disk.UniqueId
        }
    }

    # Get collection of physical disks
    $allPhysicalDisks = Get-PhysicalDisk | Where-Object {($_.BusType -EQ "SAS") -or ($_.BusType -EQ "SATA")} # -or ($_.BusType -EQ "RAID")}

    # Create a new collection of physical disks without any system/boot disks
    $physicalDisks = @()
    foreach ($physicalDisk in $allPhysicalDisks)
    {
        $addDisk = $true

        foreach ($diskIdToRemove in $diskIdsToRemove)
        {
            if ($physicalDisk.UniqueId -eq $diskIdToRemove)
            {
                $addDisk = $false
            }
        }

        if ($addDisk)
```

```powershell
        {
            $physicalDisks += $physicalDisk
        }
    }

    # Iterate through all remaining physcial disks and wipe
    Write-Host "Cleaning disks" -ForegroundColor Cyan -NoNewline
    Write-Host "..."
    $totalDisks = $physicalDisks.Count
    $counter = 1
    foreach ($physicalDisk in $physicalDisks)
    {
        $disk = $physicalDisk | Get-Disk

        # Make sure disk is Online and not ReadOnly otherwise, display reason
        # and continue
        $disk | Set-Disk -IsOffline:$false -ErrorAction SilentlyContinue
        $disk | Set-Disk -IsReadOnly:$false -ErrorAction SilentlyContinue

        # Re-instantiate disks to update changes
        $disk = $physicalDisk | Get-Disk

        if ($disk.IsOffline -or $disk.IsReadOnly)
        {
            Write-Host "Warning: " -NoNewline -ForegroundColor Yellow
            Write-Host "Unable to process disk " -NoNewline
            Write-Host $disk.Number -NoNewline
            Write-Host ": Offline Reason: " -NoNewline
            Write-Host ($disk.OfflineReason) -NoNewline -ForegroundColor Yellow
            Write-Host ", HealthStatus: " -NoNewline
            Write-Host $disk.HealthStatus -ForegroundColor Yellow
        }
        else
        {
            Write-Host "Cleaning disk " -NoNewline
            Write-Host $disk.Number -NoNewline -ForegroundColor Cyan
            Write-Host " (" -NoNewline
            Write-Host $counter -NoNewline -ForegroundColor Cyan
            Write-Host " of " -NoNewline
            Write-Host $totalDisks -NoNewline -ForegroundColor Cyan
            Write-Host ")..." -NoNewline

            # Wipe disk and initialize
            $disk | ? PartitionStyle -NE "RAW" | Clear-Disk -RemoveData -RemoveOEM -Confirm:$false
            $disk | Initialize-Disk -PartitionStyle GPT

            Write-Host Done.
        }

        $counter++
    }

    # Remove any installed roles/tools
    if ($toolsInstalled)
    {
        Write-Host Uninstalling Failover Cluster tool... -NoNewline -ForegroundColor Cyan
        Remove-WindowsFeature -Name "Failover-Clustering","RSAT-Clustering-PowerShell"
        Write-Host Done.
    }
```

```powershell
    Write-Host ""
    Write-Host "Updating the storage provider cache (x2)" -NoNewline -ForegroundColor Cyan
    Write-Host "..." -NoNewline
    Update-StorageProviderCache -DiscoveryLevel Full
    Start-Sleep 1
    Update-StorageProviderCache -DiscoveryLevel Full
    Write-Host "Done."

    # Output physical disk counts
    Write-Host ""
    Write-Host Physical Disks:
    Get-PhysicalDisk | Group-Object Manufacturer,Model,MediaType,Size | ft Count,Name -AutoSize

    Write-Host Configuration and data cleared!
    Write-Host ""
    Write-Host "Run duration: " -NoNewline
    Write-Host ([Math]::Round((([DateTime]::Now).Subtract($runStart)).TotalMinutes,2)) -ForegroundColor Yellow -NoNewline
    Write-Host " minutes"
}
```

Appendix A

BigDemo_S2D Script

As promised here is the PowerShell Script that was created for this book. Please feel free to steal it and use whatever you like for you own labs. At MVPDays sharing is everything and if we can help the community it is a huge bonus for us. Consider this our little gift for you for purchasing this book.

```
<#
Created:     2017-01-02
Version:     1.0
Author       Dave Kawula MVP and Thomas Rayner MVP
Homepage:    http://www.checkyourlogs.net

Disclaimer:
This script is provided "AS IS" with no warranties, confers no rights and
is not supported by the authors or DeploymentArtist.

Author - Dave Kawula
    Twitter: @DaveKawula
    Blog   : http://www.checkyourlogs.net

Author - Thomas Rayner
    Twitter: @MrThomasRayner
    Blog   : http://workingsysadmin.com


    .Synopsis
    Creates a big demo lab.
    .DESCRIPTION
    Huge Thank you to Ben Armstrong @VirtualPCGuy for giving me the source
starter code for this :)
    This script will build a sample lab configuration on a single Hyper-V
Server:

    It includes in this version 2 Domain Controllers, 1 x DHCP Server, 1 x MGMT
Server, 16 x S2D Nodes

    It is fully customizable as it has been created with base functions.

    The Parameters at the beginning of the script will setup the domain name,
organization name etc.

    You will need to change the <ProductKey> Variable as it has been removed for
the purposes of the print in this book.

    .EXAMPLE
    TODO: Dave, add something more meaningful in here
    .PARAMETER WorkingDir
    Transactional directory for files to be staged and written
    .PARAMETER Organization
    Org that the VMs will belong to
    .PARAMETER Owner
    Name to fill in for the OSs Owner field
```

Appendix A BigDemo_S2D Script

```powershell
    .PARAMETER TimeZone
    Timezone used by the VMs
    .PARAMETER AdminPassword
    Administrative password for the VMs
    .PARAMETER DomainName
    AD Domain to setup/join VMs to
    .PARAMETER DomainAdminPassword
    Domain recovery/admin password
    .PARAMETER VirtualSwitchName
    Name of the vSwitch for Hyper-V
    .PARAMETER Subnet
    The /24 Subnet to use for Hyper-V networking
#>

[cmdletbinding()]
param
(
    [Parameter(Mandatory)]
    [ValidateScript({ $_ -match '[^\\]$' })] #ensure WorkingDir does not end in a backslash, otherwise issues are going to come up below
    [string]
    $WorkingDir = 'c:\ClusterStoreage\Volume1\DCBuild',

    [Parameter(Mandatory)]
    [string]
    $Organization = 'MVP Rockstars',

    [Parameter(Mandatory)]
    [string]
    $Owner = 'Dave Kawula',

    [Parameter(Mandatory)]
    [ValidateScript({ $_ -in ([System.TimeZoneInfo]::GetSystemTimeZones()).ID })] #ensure a valid TimeZone was passed
    [string]
    $Timezone = 'Pacific Standard Time',

    [Parameter(Mandatory)]
    [string]
    $adminPassword = 'P@ssw0rd',

    [Parameter(Mandatory)]
    [string]
    $domainName = 'MVPDays.Com',

    [Parameter(Mandatory)]
    [string]
    $domainAdminPassword = 'P@ssw0rd',

    [Parameter(Mandatory)]
    [string]
    $virtualSwitchName = 'Dave MVP Demo',

    [Parameter(Mandatory)]
    [ValidatePattern('(\d{1,3}\.){3}')] #ensure that Subnet is formatted like the first three octets of an IPv4 address
    [string]
    $Subnet = '172.16.200.',

    [Parameter(Mandatory)]
    [string]
    $ExtraLabfilesSource = 'C:\ClusterStorage\Volume1\DCBuild\Extralabfiles'
```

Appendix A   BigDemo_S2D Script

```powershell
)
#region Functions
function Wait-PSDirect
{
    param
    (
        [string]
        $VMName,

        [Object]
        $cred
    )

    Write-Log $VMName "Waiting for PowerShell Direct (using $($cred.username))"
    while ((Invoke-Command -VMName $VMName -Credential $cred {
                'Test'
    } -ea SilentlyContinue) -ne 'Test')
    {
        Start-Sleep -Seconds 1
    }
}

Function Wait-Sleep {
            param (
                        [int]$sleepSeconds = 60,
                        [string]$title = "... Waiting for $sleepSeconds Seconds... Be Patient",
                        [string]$titleColor = "Yellow"
            )
            Write-Host -ForegroundColor $titleColor $title
            for ($sleep = 1; $sleep -le $sleepSeconds; $sleep++ ) {
                        Write-Progress -ParentId -1 -Id 42 -Activity "Sleeping for $sleepSeconds seconds" -Status "Slept for $sleep Seconds:" -percentcomplete (($sleep / $sleepSeconds) * 100)
                        Start-Sleep 1
            }
    Write-Progress -Completed -Id 42 -Activity "Done Sleeping"
    }

function Restart-DemoVM
{
    param
    (
        [string]
        $VMName
    )

    Write-Log $VMName 'Rebooting'
    stop-vm $VMName
    start-vm $VMName
}

function Confirm-Path
{
    param
    (
        [string] $path
    )
```

Appendix A BigDemo_S2D Script

```powershell
    if (!(Test-Path $path))
    {
        $null = mkdir $path
    }
}
function Write-Log
{
    param
    (
        [string]$systemName,
        [string]$message
    )

    Write-Host -Object (Get-Date).ToShortTimeString() -ForegroundColor Cyan -NoNewline
    Write-Host -Object ' - [' -ForegroundColor White -NoNewline
    Write-Host -Object $systemName -ForegroundColor Yellow -NoNewline
    Write-Host -Object "]::$($message)" -ForegroundColor White
}
function Clear-File
{
    param
    (
        [string] $file
    )

    if (Test-Path $file)
    {
        $null = Remove-Item $file -Recurse
    }
}
function Get-UnattendChunk
{
    param
    (
        [string] $pass,
        [string] $component,
        [xml]    $unattend
    )

    return $unattend.unattend.settings |
    Where-Object -Property pass -EQ -Value $pass `
    |
    Select-Object -ExpandProperty component `
    |
    Where-Object -Property name -EQ -Value $component
}
function New-UnattendFile
{
    param
    (
        [string] $filePath
    )

    # Reload template - clone is necessary as PowerShell thinks this is a "complex" object
    $unattend = $unattendSource.Clone()

    # Customize unattend XML
```

Appendix A   BigDemo_S2D Script

```powershell
    Get-UnattendChunk 'specialize' 'Microsoft-Windows-Shell-Setup' $unattend |
ForEach-Object -Process {
        $_.RegisteredOrganization = 'Azure Sea Class Covert Trial' #TR-Egg
    }
    Get-UnattendChunk 'specialize' 'Microsoft-Windows-Shell-Setup' $unattend |
ForEach-Object -Process {
        $_.RegisteredOwner = 'Thomas Rayner - @MrThomasRayner - workingsysadmin.com' #TR-Egg
    }
    Get-UnattendChunk 'specialize' 'Microsoft-Windows-Shell-Setup' $unattend |
ForEach-Object -Process {
        $_.TimeZone = $Timezone
    }
    Get-UnattendChunk 'oobeSystem' 'Microsoft-Windows-Shell-Setup' $unattend |
ForEach-Object -Process {
        $_.UserAccounts.AdministratorPassword.Value = $adminPassword
    }
    Get-UnattendChunk 'specialize' 'Microsoft-Windows-Shell-Setup' $unattend |
ForEach-Object -Process {
        $_.ProductKey = $WindowsKey
    }

    Clear-File $filePath
    $unattend.Save($filePath)
}

Function Initialize-BaseImage
{


    Mount-DiskImage $ServerISO
    $DVDDriveLetter = (Get-DiskImage $ServerISO | Get-Volume).DriveLetter
    Copy-Item -Path "$($DVDDriveLetter):\NanoServer\NanoServerImageGenerator\Convert-WindowsImage.ps1" -Destination "$($WorkingDir)\Convert-WindowsImage.ps1" -Force
    Import-Module -Name "$($DVDDriveLetter):\NanoServer\NanoServerImagegenerator\NanoServerImageGenerator.psm1" -Force


            if (!(Test-Path "$($BaseVHDPath)\NanoBase.vhdx"))
            {
            New-NanoServerImage -MediaPath "$($DVDDriveLetter):\" -BasePath $BaseVHDPath -TargetPath "$($BaseVHDPath)\NanoBase.vhdx" -Edition Standard -DeploymentType Guest -Compute -Clustering -AdministratorPassword (ConvertTo-SecureString $adminPassword -AsPlainText -Force)
           # New-NanoServerImage -MediaPath "$($DVDDriveLetter):\" -BasePath $BaseVDHPath -TargetPath "$($BaseVHDPath)\NanoBase.vhdx" -GuestDrivers -DeploymentType Guest -Edition Standard -Compute -Clustering -Defender -Storage -AdministratorPassword (ConvertTo-SecureString $adminPassword -AsPlainText -Force)


            }


    #Copy-Item -Path '$WorkingDir\Convert-WindowsImage.ps1' -Destination "$($WorkingDir)\Convert-WindowsImage.ps1" -Force
    New-UnattendFile "$WorkingDir\unattend.xml"

    #Build the Windows 2016 Core Base VHDx for the Lab
```

Appendix A BigDemo_S2D Script

```powershell
            if (!(Test-Path "$($BaseVHDPath)\VMServerBaseCore.vhdx"))
                    {

            Set-Location $workingdir

            # Load (aka "dot-source) the Function
            . .\Convert-WindowsImage.ps1
            # Prepare all the variables in advance (optional)
            $ConvertWindowsImageParam = @{
                SourcePath          = $ServerISO
                RemoteDesktopEnable = $True
                Passthru            = $True
                Edition             = "ServerDataCenterCore"
                VHDFormat           = "VHDX"
                SizeBytes           = 60GB
                WorkingDirectory    = $workingdir
                VHDPath             = "$($BaseVHDPath)\VMServerBaseCore.vhdx"
                DiskLayout          = 'UEFI'
                UnattendPath        = "$($workingdir)\unattend.xml"
            }

            $VHDx = Convert-WindowsImage @ConvertWindowsImageParam

            }


            #Build the Windows 2016 Full UI Base VHDx for the Lab

            if (!(Test-Path "$($BaseVHDPath)\VMServerBase.vhdx"))
                    {

            Set-Location $workingdir

            # Load (aka "dot-source) the Function
            . .\Convert-WindowsImage.ps1
            # Prepare all the variables in advance (optional)
            $ConvertWindowsImageParam = @{
                SourcePath          = $ServerISO
                RemoteDesktopEnable = $True
                Passthru            = $True
                Edition             = "ServerDataCenter"
                VHDFormat           = "VHDX"
                SizeBytes           = 60GB
                WorkingDirectory    = $workingdir
                VHDPath             = "$($BaseVHDPath)\VMServerBase.vhdx"
                DiskLayout          = 'UEFI'
                UnattendPath        = "$($workingdir)\unattend.xml"
            }

            $VHDx = Convert-WindowsImage @ConvertWindowsImageParam

            }

    Clear-File "$($BaseVHDPath)\unattend.xml"
    Dismount-DiskImage $ServerISO
    Clear-File "$($WorkingDir)\Convert-WindowsImage.ps1"

}
```

Appendix A BigDemo_S2D Script

```powershell
function Invoke-DemoVMPrep
{
    param
    (
        [string] $VMName,
        [string] $GuestOSName,
        [switch] $FullServer
    )

    Write-Log $VMName 'Removing old VM'
    get-vm $VMName -ErrorAction SilentlyContinue |
    stop-vm -TurnOff -Force -Passthru |
    remove-vm -Force
    Clear-File "$($VMPath)\$($GuestOSName).vhdx"

    Write-Log $VMName 'Creating new differencing disk'
    if ($FullServer)
    {
        $null = New-VHD -Path "$($VMPath)\$($GuestOSName).vhdx" -ParentPath "$($BaseVHDPath)\VMServerBase.vhdx" -Differencing
    }

    else
    {
        $null = New-VHD -Path "$($VMPath)\$($GuestOSName).vhdx" -ParentPath "$($BaseVHDPath)\VMServerBaseCore.vhdx" -Differencing
    }

    Write-Log $VMName 'Creating virtual machine'
    new-vm -Name $VMName -MemoryStartupBytes 4GB -SwitchName $virtualSwitchName `
    -Generation 2 -Path "$($VMPath)\" | Set-VM -ProcessorCount 2

    Set-VMFirmware -VMName $VMName -SecureBootTemplate MicrosoftUEFICertificateAuthority
    Set-VMFirmware -Vmname $VMName -EnableSecureBoot off
    Add-VMHardDiskDrive -VMName $VMName -Path "$($VMPath)\$($GuestOSName).vhdx" -ControllerType SCSI
    Write-Log $VMName 'Starting virtual machine'
    Enable-VMIntegrationService -Name 'Guest Service Interface' -VMName $VMName
    start-vm $VMName
}

function Create-DemoVM
{
    param
    (
        [string] $VMName,
        [string] $GuestOSName,
        [string] $IPNumber = '0'
    )

    Wait-PSDirect $VMName -cred $localCred

    Invoke-Command -VMName $VMName -Credential $localCred {
        param($IPNumber, $GuestOSName, $VMName, $domainName, $Subnet)
        if ($IPNumber -ne '0')
        {
            Write-Output -InputObject "[$($VMName)]:: Setting IP Address to $($Subnet)$($IPNumber)"
            $null = New-NetIPAddress -IPAddress "$($Subnet)$($IPNumber)" -InterfaceAlias 'Ethernet' -PrefixLength 24
            Write-Output -InputObject "[$($VMName)]:: Setting DNS Address"
```

Appendix A   BigDemo_S2D Script

```powershell
            Get-DnsClientServerAddress | ForEach-Object -Process {
                Set-DnsClientServerAddress -InterfaceIndex $_.InterfaceIndex -ServerAddresses "$($Subnet)1"
            }
        }
        Write-Output -InputObject "[$($VMName)]:: Renaming OS to `"$($GuestOSName)`""
        Rename-Computer -NewName $GuestOSName
        Write-Output -InputObject "[$($VMName)]:: Configuring WSMAN Trusted hosts"
        Set-Item -Path WSMan:\localhost\Client\TrustedHosts -Value "*.$($domainName)" -Force
        Set-Item WSMan:\localhost\client\trustedhosts "$($Subnet)*" -Force -concatenate
        Enable-WSManCredSSP -Role Client -DelegateComputer "*.$($domainName)" -Force
    } -ArgumentList $IPNumber, $GuestOSName, $VMName, $domainName, $Subnet

    Restart-DemoVM $VMName

    Wait-PSDirect $VMName -cred $localCred
}
function Invoke-NodeStorageBuild
{
    param($VMName, $GuestOSName)

    Create-DemoVM $VMName $GuestOSName
    Clear-File "$($VMPath)\$($GuestOSName) - Data 1.vhdx"
    Clear-File "$($VMPath)\$($GuestOSName) - Data 2.vhdx"
    Get-VM $VMName | Stop-VM
    Add-VMNetworkAdapter -VMName $VMName -SwitchName $virtualSwitchName
    new-vhd -Path "$($VMPath)\$($GuestOSName) - Data 1.vhdx" -Dynamic -SizeBytes 200GB
    Add-VMHardDiskDrive -VMName $VMName -Path "$($VMPath)\$($GuestOSName) - Data 1.vhdx" -ControllerType SCSI
    new-vhd -Path "$($VMPath)\$($GuestOSName) - Data 2.vhdx" -Dynamic -SizeBytes 200GB
    Add-VMHardDiskDrive -VMName $VMName -Path "$($VMPath)\$($GuestOSName) - Data 2.vhdx" -ControllerType SCSI
    Set-VMProcessor -VMName $VMName -Count 2 -ExposeVirtualizationExtensions $true
    Add-VMNetworkAdapter -VMName $VMName -SwitchName $virtualSwitchName
    Add-VMNetworkAdapter -VMName $VMName -SwitchName $virtualSwitchName
    Add-VMNetworkAdapter -VMName $VMName -SwitchName $virtualSwitchName
    Get-VMNetworkAdapter -VMName $VMName | Set-VMNetworkAdapter -AllowTeaming On
    Get-VMNetworkAdapter -VMName $VMName | Set-VMNetworkAdapter -MacAddressSpoofing on
    Start-VM $VMName
    Wait-PSDirect $VMName -cred $localCred

    Invoke-Command -VMName $VMName -Credential $localCred {
        param($VMName, $domainCred, $domainName)
        Write-Output -InputObject "[$($VMName)]:: Installing Clustering"
        $null = Install-WindowsFeature -Name File-Services, Failover-Clustering, Hyper-V -IncludeManagementTools
        Write-Output -InputObject "[$($VMName)]:: Joining domain as `"$($env:computername)`""
        while (!(Test-Connection -ComputerName $domainName -BufferSize 16 -Count 1 -Quiet -ea SilentlyContinue))
        {
            Start-Sleep -Seconds 1
        }
        do
```

Appendix A BigDemo_S2D Script

```powershell
        {
            Add-Computer -DomainName $domainName -Credential $domainCred -ea SilentlyContinue
        }
            until ($?)
    } -ArgumentList $VMName, $domainCred, $domainName

    Wait-PSDirect $VMName -cred $domainCred

    Invoke-Command -VMName $VMName -Credential $domainCred {
        Rename-NetAdapter -Name 'Ethernet' -NewName 'LOM-P0'
    }
    Invoke-Command -VMName $VMName -Credential $DomainCred {
        Rename-NetAdapter -Name 'Ethernet 2' -NewName 'LOM-P1'
    }
    Invoke-Command -VMName $VMName -Credential $DomainCred {
        Rename-NetAdapter -Name 'Ethernet 3' -NewName 'Riser-P0'
    }
    Invoke-Command -VMName $VMName -Credential $DomainCred{
        Get-NetAdapter -Name 'Ethernet 5' | Rename-NetAdapter -NewName 'Riser-P1'
    }
    Invoke-Command -VMName $VMName -Credential $DomainCred {
        New-NetLbfoTeam -Name HyperVTeam -TeamMembers 'LOM-P0' -verbose -confirm:$false
    }
    Invoke-Command -VMName $VMName -Credential $DomainCred {
        Add-NetLbfoTeamMember 'LOM-P1' -team HyperVTeam -confirm:$false
    }
    Invoke-Command -VMName $VMName -Credential $DomainCred {
        New-NetLbfoTeam -Name StorageTeam -TeamMembers 'Riser-P0' -verbose -confirm:$false
    }
    Invoke-Command -VMName $VMName -Credential $DomainCred {
        Add-NetLbfoTeamMember 'Riser-P1' -team StorageTeam -confirm:$false
    }

    Restart-DemoVM $VMName
    Wait-PSDirect $VMName -cred $domainCred

    ping localhost -n 20

    Invoke-Command -VMName $VMName -Credential $domainCred {
        New-VMSwitch -Name 'VSW01' -NetAdapterName 'HyperVTeam' -AllowManagementOS $false
    }
    Invoke-Command -VMName $VMName -Credential $domainCred {
        Add-VMNetworkAdapter -ManagementOS -Name ClusterCSV-VLAN204 -Switchname VSW01 -verbose
    }
    Invoke-Command -VMName $VMName -Credential $domainCred {
        Add-VMNetworkAdapter -ManagementOS -Name LM-VLAN203 -Switchname VSW01 -verbose
    }
    Invoke-Command -VMName $VMName -Credential $domainCred {
        Add-VMNetworkAdapter -ManagementOS -Name Servers-VLAN201 -Switchname VSW01 -verbose
    }
    Invoke-Command -VMName $VMName -Credential $domainCred {
        Add-VMNetworkAdapter -ManagementOS -Name MGMT-VLAN200 -Switchname VSW01 -verbose
    }
```

Appendix A   BigDemo_S2D Script

```powershell
    # Restart-DemoVM $VMName
}




#endregion

#region Variable Init
$BaseVHDPath = "$($WorkingDir)\BaseVHDs"
$VMPath = "$($WorkingDir)\VMs"

$localCred = New-Object -TypeName System.Management.Automation.PSCredential `
-ArgumentList 'Administrator', (ConvertTo-SecureString -String $adminPassword -
AsPlainText -Force)

$domainCred = New-Object -TypeName System.Management.Automation.PSCredential `
-ArgumentList "$($domainName)\Administrator", (ConvertTo-SecureString -String
$domainAdminPassword -AsPlainText -Force)

#$ServerISO = "D:\DCBuild\10586.0.151029-
1700.TH2_RELEASE_SERVER_OEMRET_X64FRE_EN-US.ISO"
#$ServerISO = "d:\DCBuild\14393.0.160808-
1702.RS1_Release_srvmedia_SERVER_OEMRET_X64FRE_EN-US.ISO"
#$ServerISO =
'D:\DCBuild\en_windows_server_2016_technical_preview_5_x64_dvd_8512312.iso'
$ServerISO =
'c:\ClusterStorage\Volume1\DCBuild\en_windows_server_2016_x64_dvd_9327751.iso'
#Updated for RTM Build 2016

#$WindowsKey = "2KNJJ-33Y9H-2GXGX-KMQWH-G6H67"
#$WindowsKey = '6XBNX-4JQGW-QX6QG-74P76-72V67'
$WindowsKey = 'QJP9N-Q6RY7-VTP6Y-2MTF8-BWR7R' #Dave's Technet KEY Remove for
Publishing of Book

$unattendSource = [xml]@"
<?xml version="1.0" encoding="utf-8"?>
<unattend xmlns="urn:schemas-microsoft-com:unattend">
    <servicing></servicing>
    <settings pass="specialize">
        <component name="Microsoft-Windows-Shell-Setup"
processorArchitecture="amd64" publicKeyToken="31bf3856ad364e35"
language="neutral" versionScope="nonSxS"
xmlns:wcm="http://schemas.microsoft.com/WMIConfig/2002/State"
xmlns:xsi="http://www.w3.org/2001/XMLSchema-instance">
            <ComputerName>*</ComputerName>
            <ProductKey>2KNJJ-33Y9H-2GXGX-KMQWH-G6H67</ProductKey>
            <RegisteredOrganization>Organization</RegisteredOrganization>
            <RegisteredOwner>Owner</RegisteredOwner>
            <TimeZone>TZ</TimeZone>
        </component>
    </settings>
    <settings pass="oobeSystem">
        <component name="Microsoft-Windows-Shell-Setup"
processorArchitecture="amd64" publicKeyToken="31bf3856ad364e35"
language="neutral" versionScope="nonSxS"
xmlns:wcm="http://schemas.microsoft.com/WMIConfig/2002/State"
xmlns:xsi="http://www.w3.org/2001/XMLSchema-instance">
            <OOBE>
                <HideEULAPage>true</HideEULAPage>
                <HideLocalAccountScreen>true</HideLocalAccountScreen>
                <HideWirelessSetupInOOBE>true</HideWirelessSetupInOOBE>
```

```xml
                <NetworkLocation>Work</NetworkLocation>
                <ProtectYourPC>1</ProtectYourPC>
            </OOBE>
            <UserAccounts>
                <AdministratorPassword>
                    <Value>password</Value>
                    <PlainText>True</PlainText>
                </AdministratorPassword>
            </UserAccounts>
        </component>
        <component name="Microsoft-Windows-International-Core" processorArchitecture="amd64" publicKeyToken="31bf3856ad364e35" language="neutral" versionScope="nonSxS" xmlns:wcm="http://schemas.microsoft.com/WMIConfig/2002/State" xmlns:xsi="http://www.w3.org/2001/XMLSchema-instance">
            <InputLocale>en-us</InputLocale>
            <SystemLocale>en-us</SystemLocale>
            <UILanguage>en-us</UILanguage>
            <UILanguageFallback>en-us</UILanguageFallback>
            <UserLocale>en-us</UserLocale>
        </component>
    </settings>
</unattend>
"@
#endregion
```

```powershell
Write-Log 'Host' 'Getting started...'

Confirm-Path $BaseVHDPath
Confirm-Path $VMPath
Write-Log 'Host' 'Building Base Images'

if (!(Test-Path -Path "$($BaseVHDPath)\VMServerBase.vhdx"))
{
    . Initialize-BaseImage
}

if ((Get-VMSwitch | Where-Object -Property name -EQ -Value $virtualSwitchName) -eq $null)
{
    New-VMSwitch -Name $virtualSwitchName -SwitchType Private
}

Invoke-DemoVMPrep 'Domain Controller 1' 'DC1' -FullServer
Invoke-DemoVMPrep 'Domain Controller 2' 'DC2' -FullServer
Invoke-DemoVMPrep 'DHCP Server' 'DHCP' -FullServer
Invoke-DemoVMPrep 'Management Console' 'Management' -FullServer

$VMName = 'Domain Controller 1'
$GuestOSName = 'DC1'
$IPNumber = '1'

Create-DemoVM $VMName $GuestOSName $IPNumber

Invoke-Command -VMName $VMName -Credential $localCred {
    param($VMName, $domainName, $domainAdminPassword)

    Write-Output -InputObject "[$($VMName)]:: Installing AD"
    $null = Install-WindowsFeature AD-Domain-Services -IncludeManagementTools
    Write-Output -InputObject "[$($VMName)]:: Enabling Active Directory and promoting to domain controller"
```

Appendix A BigDemo_S2D Script

```powershell
        Install-ADDSForest -DomainName $domainName -InstallDNS -NoDNSonNetwork `
-NoRebootOnCompletion `
            -SafeModeAdministratorPassword (ConvertTo-SecureString -String
$domainAdminPassword -AsPlainText -Force) -confirm:$false
} -ArgumentList $VMName, $domainName, $domainAdminPassword

Restart-DemoVM $VMName


$VMName = 'DHCP Server'
$GuestOSName = 'DHCP'
$IPNumber = '3'

Create-DemoVM $VMName $GuestOSName $IPNumber

Invoke-Command -VMName $VMName -Credential $localCred {
    param($VMName, $domainCred, $domainName)
    Write-Output -InputObject "[$($VMName)]:: Installing DHCP"
    $null = Install-WindowsFeature DHCP -IncludeManagementTools
    Write-Output -InputObject "[$($VMName)]:: Joining domain as
`"$($env:computername)`""
    while (!(Test-Connection -ComputerName $domainName -BufferSize 16 -Count 1 -
Quiet -ea SilentlyContinue))
    {
        Start-Sleep -Seconds 1
    }
    do
    {
        Add-Computer -DomainName $domainName -Credential $domainCred -ea
SilentlyContinue
    }
    until ($?)
} -ArgumentList $VMName, $domainCred, $domainName

Restart-DemoVM $VMName
Wait-PSDirect $VMName -cred $domainCred

Invoke-Command -VMName $VMName -Credential $domainCred {
    param($VMName, $domainName, $Subnet, $IPNumber)

    Write-Output -InputObject "[$($VMName)]:: Waiting for name resolution"

    while ((Test-NetConnection -ComputerName $domainName).PingSucceeded -eq
$false)
    {
        Start-Sleep -Seconds 1
    }

    Write-Output -InputObject "[$($VMName)]:: Configuring DHCP Server"
    Set-DhcpServerv4Binding -BindingState $true -InterfaceAlias Ethernet
    Add-DhcpServerv4Scope -Name 'IPv4 Network' -StartRange "$($Subnet)10" -
EndRange "$($Subnet)200" -SubnetMask 255.255.255.0
    Set-DhcpServerv4OptionValue -OptionId 6 -value "$($Subnet)1"
    Add-DhcpServerInDC -DnsName "$($env:computername).$($domainName)"
    foreach($i in 1..99)
    {
        $mac = '00-b5-5d-fe-f6-' + ($i % 100).ToString('00')
        $ip = $Subnet + '1' + ($i % 100).ToString('00')
        $desc = 'Container ' + $i.ToString()
        $scopeID = $Subnet + '0'
        Add-DhcpServerv4Reservation -IPAddress $ip -ClientId $mac -Description
$desc -ScopeId $scopeID
    }
```

Appendix A BigDemo_S2D Script

```powershell
    } -ArgumentList $VMName, $domainName, $Subnet, $IPNumber

    Restart-DemoVM $VMName

    $VMName = 'Domain Controller 2'
    $GuestOSName = 'DC2'
    $IPNumber = '2'

    Create-DemoVM $VMName $GuestOSName $IPNumber

    Invoke-Command -VMName $VMName -Credential $localCred {
        param($VMName, $domainCred, $domainName)
        Write-Output -InputObject "[$($VMName)]:: Installing AD"
        $null = Install-WindowsFeature AD-Domain-Services -IncludeManagementTools
        Write-Output -InputObject "[$($VMName)]:: Joining domain as `"$($env:computername)`""
        while (!(Test-Connection -ComputerName $domainName -BufferSize 16 -Count 1 -Quiet -ea SilentlyContinue))
        {
            Start-Sleep -Seconds 1
        }
        do
        {
            Add-Computer -DomainName $domainName -Credential $domainCred -ea SilentlyContinue
        }
        until ($?)
    } -ArgumentList $VMName, $domainCred, $domainName

    Restart-DemoVM $VMName
    Wait-PSDirect $VMName -cred $domainCred

    Invoke-Command -VMName $VMName -Credential $domainCred {
        param($VMName, $domainName, $domainAdminPassword)

        Write-Output -InputObject "[$($VMName)]:: Waiting for name resolution"

        while ((Test-NetConnection -ComputerName $domainName).PingSucceeded -eq $false)
        {
            Start-Sleep -Seconds 1
        }

        Write-Output -InputObject "[$($VMName)]:: Enabling Active Directory and promoting to domain controller"

        Install-ADDSDomainController -DomainName $domainName -InstallDNS -NoRebootOnCompletion `
            -SafeModeAdministratorPassword (ConvertTo-SecureString -String $domainAdminPassword -AsPlainText -Force) -confirm:$false
    } -ArgumentList $VMName, $domainName, $domainAdminPassword

    Restart-DemoVM $VMName

    $VMName = 'Domain Controller 1'
    $GuestOSName = 'DC1'
    $IPNumber = '1'

    Wait-PSDirect $VMName -cred $domainCred

    Invoke-Command -VMName $VMName -Credential $domainCred {
        param($VMName, $password)
```

Appendix A BigDemo_S2D Script

```powershell
    Write-Output -InputObject "[$($VMName)]:: Creating user account for Dave"
    do
    {
        Start-Sleep -Seconds 5
        New-ADUser `
        -Name 'Dave' `
        -SamAccountName 'Dave' `
        -DisplayName 'Dave' `
        -AccountPassword (ConvertTo-SecureString -String $password -AsPlainText -Force) `
        -ChangePasswordAtLogon $false `
        -Enabled $true -ea 0
    }
    until ($?)
    Add-ADGroupMember -Identity 'Domain Admins' -Members 'Dave'
} -ArgumentList $VMName, $domainAdminPassword

$VMName = 'Management Console'
$GuestOSName = 'Management'

Create-DemoVM $VMName $GuestOSName

Invoke-Command -VMName $VMName -Credential $localCred {
    param($VMName, $domainCred, $domainName)
    Write-Output -InputObject "[$($VMName)]:: Management tools"
    $null = Install-WindowsFeature RSAT-Clustering, RSAT-Hyper-V-Tools
    Write-Output -InputObject "[$($VMName)]:: Joining domain as `"$($env:computername)`""
    while (!(Test-Connection -ComputerName $domainName -BufferSize 16 -Count 1 -Quiet -ea SilentlyContinue))
    {
        Start-Sleep -Seconds 1
    }
    do
    {
        Add-Computer -DomainName $domainName -Credential $domainCred -ea SilentlyContinue
    }
    until ($?)
} -ArgumentList $VMName, $domainCred, $domainName

Restart-DemoVM $VMName
#Wait-PSDirect $VMName

Invoke-DemoVMPrep 'S2DNode1' 'S2DNode1' -FullServer
Invoke-DemoVMPrep 'S2DNode2' 'S2DNode2' -FullServer
Invoke-DemoVMPrep 'S2DNode3' 'S2DNode3' -FullServer
Invoke-DemoVMPrep 'S2DNode4' 'S2DNode4' -FullServer
Invoke-DemoVMPrep 'S2DNode5' 'S2DNode5' -FullServer
Invoke-DemoVMPrep 'S2DNode6' 'S2DNode6' -FullServer
Invoke-DemoVMPrep 'S2DNode7' 'S2DNode7' -FullServer
Invoke-DemoVMPrep 'S2DNode8' 'S2DNode8' -FullServer

Wait-PSDirect 'S2DNode8' -cred $localCred

$VMName = 'S2DNode1'
$GuestOSName = 'S2Dnode1'

Invoke-NodeStorageBuild 'S2DNode1' 'S2DNode1'
Invoke-NodeStorageBuild 'S2DNode2' 'S2DNode2'
Invoke-NodeStorageBuild 'S2DNode3' 'S2DNode3'
Invoke-NodeStorageBuild 'S2DNode4' 'S2DNode4'
```

Appendix A BigDemo_S2D Script

```powershell
    Invoke-NodeStorageBuild 'S2DNode5' 'S2DNode5'
    Invoke-NodeStorageBuild 'S2DNode6' 'S2DNode6'
    Invoke-NodeStorageBuild 'S2DNode7' 'S2DNode7'
    Invoke-NodeStorageBuild 'S2DNode8' 'S2DNode8'


Wait-PSDirect 'S2DNode8' -cred $domainCred

Invoke-Command -VMName 'Management Console' -Credential $domainCred {
    param ($domainName)
    do
    {
        New-Cluster -Name S2DCluster -Node S2DNode1, S2DNode2, S2DNode3, S2DNode4,S2DNode5,S2DNode6,S2DNode7,S2DNode8 -NoStorage
    }
    until ($?)
    while (!(Test-Connection -ComputerName "S2DCluster.$($domainName)" -BufferSize 16 -Count 1 -Quiet -ea SilentlyContinue))
    {
        ipconfig.exe /flushdns
        Start-Sleep -Seconds 1
    }
    #Enable-ClusterStorageSpacesDirect -Cluster "S2DCluster.$($domainName)"
    #Add-ClusterScaleOutFileServerRole -name S2DFileServer -cluster "S2DCluster.$($domainName)"
} -ArgumentList $domainName

Invoke-Command -VMName 'S2DNode1' -Credential $domainCred {
    param ($domainName)
    #New-StoragePool -StorageSubSystemName "S2DCluster.$($domainName)" -FriendlyName S2DPool -WriteCacheSizeDefault 0 -ProvisioningTypeDefault Fixed -ResiliencySettingNameDefault Mirror -PhysicalDisk (Get-StorageSubSystem  -Name "S2DCluster.$($domainName)" | Get-PhysicalDisk)
    #New-Volume -StoragePoolFriendlyName S2DPool -FriendlyName S2DDisk -PhysicalDiskRedundancy 2 -FileSystem CSVFS_REFS -Size 500GB
    #updated from MSFT TP5 notes

    # The Cmdlet changed for RTM - Enable-ClusterS2D -CacheMode Disabled -AutoConfig:0 -SkipEligibilityChecks -confirm:$false
    #This step can take a little while espeically if you are adding a lot of nodes and disks
    Enable-ClusterStorageSpacesDirect -PoolFriendlyName S2DPool -confirm:$False

    #Create storage pool and set media type to HDD
    #New-StoragePool -StorageSubSystemFriendlyName *Cluster* -FriendlyName S2D -ProvisioningTypeDefault Fixed -PhysicalDisk (Get-PhysicalDisk | Where-Object -Property CanPool -EQ -Value $true)

    #Create a volume
    #This will match the configuration that was done in the book

    New-Volume -StoragePoolFriendlyName S2DPool -FriendlyName Mirror-2Way -FileSystem CSVFS_REFS -Size 200GB -PhysicalDiskRedundancy 1
    New-Volume -StoragePoolFriendlyName S2DPool -FriendlyName Mirror-3Way -FileSystem CSVFS_REFS -Size 200GB -PhysicalDiskRedundancy 2

} -ArgumentList $domainName

Write-Log 'Done' 'Done!'
```

Appendix A   BigDemo_S2D Script

Join us at MVPDays and meet great MVP's like this in person

If you liked this book, you will love to hear them in person.

Live Presentations

Dave frequently speaks at Microsoft conferences around North America, such as TechEd, VeeamOn, TechDays, and MVPDays Community Roadshow.

Cristal runs the MVPDays Community Roadshow.

You can find additional information on the following blog:

> www.checkyourlogs.net
>
> www.mvpdays.com

Video Training

For video-based training, see the following site:

> www.mvpdays.com

Live Instructor-led Classes

Dave has been a Microsoft Certified Trainer (MCT) for more than 15 years and presents scheduled instructor-led classes in the US and Canada. For current dates and locations, see the following sites:

- www.truesec.com
- www.checkyourlogs.net

Find our Experts   Join us at MVPDays and meet great MVP's like this in person

Consulting Services

Dave and Cristal have worked with some of the largest companies in the world and have a wealth of experience and expertise. Customer engagements are typically between two weeks and six months. For more information, see the following site:

www.triconelite.com and www.rsvccorp.com

Twitter

Dave, Cristal, Émile, Thomas, Allan, and Clint are on Twitter using the following aliases:

- Dave Kawula: @DaveKawula
- Cristal Kawula: @SuperCristal1
- Émile Cabot: @Ecabot
- Thomas Rayner: @MrThomasRayner
- Allan Rafuse: @AllanRafuse
- Clint Wyckoff: @ClintWyckoff

You can also follow:

- MVPDays: @MVPDays
- MVPHour: #MVPHour
- Data_Raft: @Data_RAFT

Made in the USA
Columbia, SC
14 October 2017